MUNCH
LUNCH
— & —
DINNER

Delicious and
Nutritious
Recipes for
Budget Friendly,
Eco-conscious
Cooking

MARY LOUISE NEEDHAM-CARLTON

Cover image by: Usman Tariq 99D
Book design by: SWATT Books Ltd

Printed in the United Kingdom
First Printing, 2023

ISBN: 978-1-7390887-0-5 (Hardback)
ISBN: 978-1-7390887-2-9 (Paperback)
ISBN: 978-1-7390887-1-2 (eBook)

Mary Louise Needham-Carlton
Ovington, Hampshire

www.munchcic.co.uk

Acknowledgements

Food photography: Cath Lowe Photography
Supported by Winchester City Council

Our thanks to everyone who volunteers at, supports and attends our Munch clubs! You are all amazing ☺

Contents

Introduction

At Munch we believe everyone should have access to good healthy food. From being able to afford financially a balanced, nutritious diet to having the skills to cook it, we believe in empowering people, individuals, families and communities, to eat well and live well.

In a world where we are bombarded with celebrity chefs, social media and aspirational cooking, we aim to help people learn about simple, everyday food, to take the fear out of cooking and help people to develop the skills and confidence they need to cook from scratch.

We are passionate about fighting health inequalities, empowering communities, and helping individuals make healthy changes and learn about sustainable nutrition.

Munch is a community interest company based in Winchester, Hampshire. We create bespoke events catering, all profits of which go towards supporting our community workshops.

Our Community Cooking programme offers fun, structured, fully inclusive workshops for families with children, teenagers, adults with learning disabilities, and disadvantaged groups.

We run sessions both online and in person, where we help people build a healthy relationship with food, adopt a sustainable approach to eating, strengthen financial resilience and waste less.

You can find out more about Munch at www.munchcic.co.uk. If you would like to be involved in what we do, we would love to hear from you.

The recipes in this book have all been tried and tested by a broad range of people in our Munch clubs and have all been proven to be:

⟩ quick and easy to follow and to cook, with no specialist knowledge required
⟩ full of nutritious, affordable and easy-to-obtain ingredients
⟩ ideal for all the family

We hope that the recipes will help you make some changes towards a flexible, more plant-based diet, for your health and for your world.

Omnivore? Herbivore? Flexitarian?

An omnivore, as you may or may not know, is a creature that eats both plants and animals; the word comes from the Latin, *omnis* – meaning *everything* – and vorare, meaning *to devour or eat*. Most people in the Western (first) World are omnivores, eating a combination of meat, fish, dairy, fruit, seeds, nuts and vegetables.

A herbivore is a creature that can survive only on plants; a human herbivore is commonly known as a vegan, someone who has made a conscious decision to only eat plant-based foods.

A flexitarian is a modern term which refers to someone who is essentially an omnivore but one who chooses to consume a high proportion of plant-based foods and only a minimal amount of meat, fish and dairy products.

A vegan diet is commonly thought of as the most environmentally friendly diet, whereas the omnivore is seen to be the most detrimental to the environment. This is mainly due to the high meat and dairy consumption that many omnivores indulge in. In fact, a lot of omnivores, literally do *devour everything*!

Animal production for food is responsible for a disproportionately high percentage of agriculture's greenhouse gas (GHG) emissions. About 20% is from the farming element – land, water, feed – and about 10% is from slaughtering, processing, packaging and waste. So, in total, one third of GHG is from meat and dairy production, surely unsustainable as the climate disaster increases. Cattle production (beef and dairy) is responsible for the highest greenhouse gas (GHG) emissions in

farming, which is ironic, considering that cattle are herbivores.

So, should we all become herbivores? Not necessarily. The vegan lifestyle is drastic and absolutely not for everybody, as eating a suitable level of protein can be a challenge. Plus, depending on how informed (or uninformed) you are in how you follow a vegan diet, you may end up contributing to high GHG emissions in different ways.

For example, someone following a plant-based diet who is eating high amounts of air freighted fruits and vegetables, or a lot of nuts, which require a huge amount of water to be produced, is likely to have a higher climate impact than a well-informed flexitarian, one who only cooks from scratch using local, seasonal produce.

We need to remember that our dietary environmental impact is not just based on what we eat but is also about where our food has come from, how it has got to us, how it is produced, how it is processed, how it is packaged, how we cook it, how we store it, whether we eat it or whether we bin it.

A minefield right?!

Well, no, it doesn't have to be.

While the evidence suggests that switching to a vegan diet is the most effective way of reducing our GHG emissions, it also shows that reducing our energy (calorie) intake and adopting a healthier (flexitarian) diet comes a very close second[1]. This recipe book is flexitarian, in that it is not purely vegetarian, but there are NO beef recipes. Instead, the focus is on poultry and fish (chicken, turkey, tuna and mackerel), therefore using more planet-friendly sources of protein.

So, in fact it's easy - the way we look after our planet starts with the way we look after ourselves.

---

1   Hallström, E., Carlsson-Kanyama, A., and Börjesson, P. (2015). Environmental impact of dietary change: a systematic review. *Journal of Cleaner Production, 91(0), 1-11*

The Good Life versus the reality: Getting it right

Perhaps we would all like to grow our own food, perhaps we wouldn't, but the reality is that a lot of people just can't.

Growing your own food requires space, time, energy, persistence, good mobility, a little bit of knowledge and a fair amount of disappointment when the slugs eat your tomatoes that you have been lovingly growing from seed and nurturing for the past three months!

I would certainly not discourage growing your own food and I try to grow a fair amount of mine, but we must be realistic about what this involves. For most people, it would require altering their lifestyles in a way which is neither achievable nor enjoyable.

So, we must do what we can, within our own parameters.

I would encourage you to grow herbs, tomatoes and peppers on your windowsills, and if you have some space in your garden try easy things like beetroot, spring onions, potatoes and salad items. Shop-bought salad crops in particular are often grown in highly treated greenhouse environments, both in the UK and abroad, and have travelled thousands of miles, producing high levels of GHG.

Teach your children about where our food comes from, how to eat seasonally, and plant radishes and salads (things that grow quickly) with them so they can feel the magic of watching something grow!

Local, seasonal, frozen, flown

What we can also do, if we are not growing our own food, is educate ourselves on how to shop for fruit and veg in the most environmentally friendly way. This means choosing local and seasonal foods, limiting foods from greenhouses (heat and light treated), and seeking out ocean freighted rather than air freighted products.

The most healthy and sustainable way to buy fresh fruit and veg is to buy local and seasonal produce. However, local produce, say from a farm shop, tends to be expensive and out of reach for a lot of people. So, if you can't do that, try to stick with seasonal British fruit and vegetables when you can. If you are buying imported foods, try to stick with fruit and veg that has travelled by boat. Air freight generates 47 times more greenhouse gas emissions, per tonne per mile, than freight which has travelled by boat.

Helpfully for us, the fruit and veg we buy in the supermarket is always labelled with where it has travelled from; unhelpfully for us, it is not labelled with how it has travelled. The best way to work this out for yourself, is to think, *perishable* or *non-perishable*? *Non-perishable* foods, those with a longer shelf life, such as oranges, apples and bananas, travel well in the temperature-controlled hold of a boat. However, *perishable* food such as soft fruits and salad products (cucumber, tomatoes, lettuce etc) deteriorates quickly after being picked, so has to travel quickly, by air. Air-freighted fruit and veg sits in the same climate-impact category as lower impact animal products like chicken.[2]

---

2   Bridle SL (2020). *Food and Climate Change Without the Hot Air.*

The Frozen Revolution (and revelation)!

For many years there was a huge stigma around using frozen veg but now people are starting to realise the benefits – both from a health point of view and an environmental point of view.

Of course, nothing tastes as sensational as the first summer strawberries from the garden or your local pick-your-own, but once that fruit or vegetable has been picked it instantly starts to lose its nutritional value. Fruit and veg we buy in the supermarket often sits around for days before it enters our mouths! As it travels and is treated, all those essential vitamins (such as C and A) are depleting at an alarming rate. As consumers we often over-buy – as we don't want to go to the supermarket every day – and few people plan each day's meals. Instead, it often feels easier to buy a load of stuff that we think we're likely to use, but then all too often we find it at the back of the fridge days (or even weeks) later.

Household food waste accounts for a frightening 70% of the food wasted annually in the UK. On average each person in the UK wastes around 200g of food a day (worth around 66p – that's a minimum of £240 per year)[3] and the most wasted foods are fruit, vegetables and salads. So, using frozen veg makes sense, as you only use what you need. No waste, more money in your pocket, AND a higher nutritional value – this all sounds good to me!

---

3   Bridle SL (2020). *Food and Climate Change Without the Hot Air.*

Six sustainable nutrition tips

To start to make a change to how you shop, cook and eat, in ways that are healthier and more environmentally friendly, here are six tips you can follow right now and which are backed up by the recipes in this book.

1. **Cook from scratch.** This means using fresh food and ingredients you can find in your kitchen and cutting down on processed food. Processed food is worse for the environment as often huge amounts of water and energy are used in the processing. Also, processed food tends to involve loads of different ingredients, and you don't know where these ingredients are from or indeed how they are processed. Most processed food is likely to be ultra-processed — for example meat-free 'meat' products, ready meals and ready-made sauces. Ultra-processed food tends to have six or more ingredients attached to it and is likely to be high in sweeteners, preservatives, salt, artificial colours and flavourings.
   Cooking from scratch also usually means less packaging, so less waste to landfill.

2. **Lower your meat and dairy intake.** Aim to eat veggie or vegan meals at least five days out of seven.

3. **Think about how your food has got to you.** Air vs sea vs up the road! Ideally, we all should be eating in-season British fruit and vegetables (field grown) which have not been grown in a greenhouse. However, as previously mentioned, this is not realistic for everyone. Do your best to be mindful, to do what you can to follow sustainable nutrition.

4. **Get enough protein and fibre!** If you are preparing a vegan meal, make sure you combine plant sources to make a complete protein. Animal products contain all the essential proteins (amino acids), known as complete proteins, that our bodies need for healthy and efficient function, but plant products do not. However, by combining two sources of fibrous carbohydrate (nuts, seeds, pulses, rice, legumes, vegetables) you can make a complete protein. Always make sure you have two different components of fibre in your vegan meal.

5. **Eat a diet which is rich in vegetables, wholegrains, beans, pulses and legumes.**

6. **Eat mindfully, waste less, and try to cook efficiently.**

All the recipes in this book aim to help you to achieve these 6 sustainable nutrition tips.

How to use this book

Chopping glossary

Use the photo below to visualise the different styles of chopping that are described throughout the book: dice, grate, ribbon etc.

De-stalking your greens

1.

Hold the leaf flat on your chopping board with one hand placed firmly on the middle of the leaf next to the stalk.

2.

Using a small knife, carefully cut down the line of the stalk on one side.

3.

Repeat on the other side.

4.

Remove the stalk. Keep the stalks as you can use them too, by chopping up small or grating.

Spoon Guide

Serving Spoon

Dessert Spoon

Teaspoon

All the recipes in this book use standard spoon sizes as the measuring device for various ingredients, as every kitchen is likely to have these, and they are less complicated than talking about fluid ounces etc. Our abbreviations in the recipes are teaspoon = tsp and dessert spoon = dstspn.

Hob life!

Cooking in one pan on a hob is usually more economic than cooking in the oven. It is also better for the planet to try to use as little energy as possible when cooking. So, this is clearly a win, win. There is just one recipe in this book that requires an oven, with the rest just using a one-pan hob. Most of the recipes in this book can be easily adapted for a slow cooker, which is leaps and bounds the most economical way to cook.

How long does each recipe take?

You will see that none of the recipes in this book have a time indication on how long they will take to make. This is because the amount of time will vary, depending on your skill sets in chopping and preparing the ingredients, along with your experience in cooking from scratch prior to using this book. I don't know about you, but whenever I use a recipe, it always seems to take longer than the time detailed by the writer. This can be frustrating and can put you off cooking.

I would say, as a guide, that you should take no longer than 30-60 minutes to cook any of the dishes in this book; however, if you are new to cooking it may take longer. Don't let this put you off! As with everything, cooking is about learning and experience; the first time will always take longer and the more you do it the quicker you will become!

Batch cooking

If you can, I recommend cooking double amounts of a recipe and freezing portions for another time. This saves you time, money and energy - yours and your utilities!

Freeze your batches in one- or two-person portion sizes (depending on your household) so that you do not waste any when it comes to defrosting and reheating.

I would not recommend freezing accompaniments like rice or pasta, just the sauces, then cook the accompaniment from scratch when you are reheating. Batch cooking is a great way to have a healthy meal in minutes after a long day!

Remember to label your item before putting it in the freezer, so you know what it is! And put the date that you are freezing it. However, please don't freeze portions and then forget about them! Official food safety guidelines state that it is best practice that frozen food should be used by one month after it is frozen, so forward plan when you are next going to eat a batch you have frozen.

If you are putting your leftovers in the fridge, also put them in a box and put the date that the food was made on the box.

Leftovers in the fridge should be consumed by three days after the food was made.

Always defrost food thoroughly by leaving frozen items in your fridge for 24 hours or use the defrost function on your microwave.

The most economical way to reheat your food is by using a microwave, or you can reheat in a pan on the hob. Reheat until piping hot.

WASTE LESS

In this book we use a lot of frozen veg and dried herbs as well as the odd preserved food.

This is to help you waste less and just use what you need. Before I started growing my own herbs, I always bought them from the supermarket and always threw most of them in the bin before I'd had a chance to use them! Dried herbs are a great alternative.

You will also see that many of the recipes in this book use similar fresh ingredients, again to avoid food waste. Hopefully, if you have something left in your fridge from making one recipe (eg half a pepper), you will have another recipe where you can use it up.

Palm portion sizes

As a rule of thumb (excuse the pun) we recommend using your hand to measure portion sizes. You will see through this book that we use 'handfuls' for pasta, rice, vegetables and various other items. Of course, all hand sizes vary but an average handful measures about 75g of dry pasta or rice.

Often, we tend to over-portion these starch carbohydrates because when they are dry, these handful portions look very small. However, as I'm sure you know, these staples expand when cooked. You will find a handful is adequate.

This is a good way to measure portions as it saves waste and is healthier.

As a contrast you might find, when measuring veg, that a couple of handfuls looks like a lot, but here it is important to remember that the veg shrinks when cooked. Besides, there's no such thing as too much veg, right?!

Cooking oil

You will see that throughout the book we do not specify a type of oil to use. This is because we all have different preferences which might be based on price, flavour, environment or our cooking influencers.

Here we have created a comparison table of some of the more commonly used cooking oils, to help you decide which is best for you.

OIL	HEALTH BENEFITS	USE FOR	COOKING POINT	ENVIRONMENTAL IMPACT	PRICE
Extra virgin olive oil	Research suggests extra virgin olive oil is the healthiest as it is unrefined (unprocessed). High in monounsaturated fats which are better for your heart and cholesterol levels.	Cooking (frying, roasting etc), salad dressings, pesto, hummus.	For best results do not use on a high heat as the oil will burn or evaporate quickly. Stick to medium for optimal results.	The main environmental impact of olive oil comes from waste disposal of by-product and water usage. Go for organic or cold pressed, unrefined extra virgin, as there is no heating or use of chemicals. Organic producers are often more responsible in terms of waste as well.	£££
Olive oil	Similar to extra virgin but may have undergone some processing so may contain some trace chemicals like fertilizer etc.	Cooking (frying, roasting etc), salad dressings, pesto, hummus.	For best results do not use on a high heat as the oil will burn or evaporate quickly. Stick to medium for optimal results.	Olive oil creates a lot of waste by product and is also bad for the environment in terms of land degradation and water usage. [4]	££

4   Alamprese, C. Caponio, F. and Chiavaro, E. (2021). "Sustainability of the olive oil system", Foods, 10(8): 1730.

OIL	HEALTH BENEFITS	USE FOR	COOKING POINT	ENVIRONMENTAL IMPACT	PRICE
Sunflower oil	Contains vitamin E which is essential for healthy skin, eyes, and cell reproduction. High in omega-6 which should only be consumed in moderation. Sunflower oil is a good cheaper alternative to olive oil.	Cooking (frying, roasting etc)	Can use on a high or medium heat. Use sparingly.	Processing requiring fertilizers and chemicals can produce high GHG emissions. However, sunflower oil production uses relatively less water than the production of other oils.	£
Vegetable oil	"Vegetable" oils are generic, they are comprised of several different oils such as corn, palm and soy and are therefore unrefined. They are low in saturated fats.	Cooking (frying, roasting etc)	Can use on a high or medium heat. Use sparingly	Processing requiring fertilizers and chemicals can produce high GHG emissions.	£
Sesame oil	Contains monounsaturated and polyunsaturated fats, as well as vitamin E.	Cooking (frying, roasting etc)	Can use on a high or medium heat. Use sparingly	Look for 'cold-pressed' sesame oil, which does not use any chemicals in the processing.	££
Nut oils	Nut oils are tasty and high in omega-3.	Only use for garnish or dressings.	Do not cook.	Bear in mind that nut production requires a high amount of water so is not sustainable.	££

OIL	HEALTH BENEFITS	USE FOR	COOKING POINT	ENVIRONMENTAL IMPACT	PRICE
Coconut oil	Although there is some research that suggests coconut oils might be good for you – and in recent years it has been highly promoted as such – I would steer clear of it altogether as it contains high levels of saturated fat which is bad for your heart and blood.	If you must use coconut oil use it sparingly and only use for flash frying, like stir fries.	High heat	Studies in recent years have suggested that coconut production is more responsible for de-forestation than palm oil[5] posing a threat to biodiversity and 20 different species of plant and animal.	£££

5   Meijaard, E. Abrams, J. F. Juffe-Bignoli, D. Voigt, M. and Sheil, D. (2020). "Coconut oil, conservation and the conscientious consumer", Current Biology. 30(16): 3274-3275

Easy-to-read recipes

In the back of this book are easy-to-read versions of 20 of our most popular recipes. If you would like to access any of the other recipes in an easy-to-read format, please contact us via our website at www.munchcic.co.uk.

Shortcuts and timesavers

Easy chilli: Before the birth of our son fresh chilli went in everything and we always had some in the fridge. After the birth of our son chilli stopped going in everything but we still always had it in the fridge (old habits die hard) so needless it say, it often ended up in the bin! A jar of readymade Easy Chilli is a great alternative as it still tastes really fresh, and no waste!

Miso paste: A perfect alternative to stock! I used to make a lot of meat stock but now that I eat fewer things with bones, I find miso is a great substitute – it's packed full of flavour and much quicker to prepare too.

Milled seeds and whole seeds: An excellent throw into any sauce or soup, to add nutrients, fibre and texture.

Hot sauce: Although I recommend staying away from processed foods as much as possible, realistically we are unlikely to make all our own flavour condiments. Adding a dash of something here or there is very different to consuming a whole ready-meal or using a jar of ready-made pasta sauce, for example. Hot sauce adds a boost to dishes like burritos and is good if you all have different palates regarding the same dish.

WASHING YOUR HANDS

When starting out to make any of the recipes in this book, the first step always (and this is highlighted in the easy-to-read recipes further on) is to wash your hands thoroughly. And, as well as doing this before you begin, if the recipe involves handling raw poultry or fish, then wash them again after handling this. And clean down thoroughly any chopping surface you have used.

The recipes

Soups

A good soup is a complete meal in a bowl — easy and economical to make, nutritious, and warming and comforting, so the perfect set of recipes to start off with.

PEA & MINT SOUP
Makes 4 servings

Don't underestimate the mighty pea! These little powerhouses are packed with vitamin C and bursting with natural sugars. Mint is good for your digestion and will grow anywhere in abundance! Together these two are a match made in heaven and this recipe is so easy, you can make a batch and throw it in the freezer for a rainy day.

INGREDIENTS

> 2 cloves garlic
> 1 onion
> 1 dstspn of cooking oil
> 2 pinches of salt
> 1 tsp mixed herbs
> 1 sachet miso soup paste
> 3 or 4 sprigs of mint
> 3 serving spoon frozen peas
> 800 ml water

METHOD

1. Chop the mint (stalks and all) as small as you can and set to one side.
2. Peel the garlic and onion, then roughly chop.
3. Heat your oil, on a medium heat, in a medium sized saucepan.
4. Add the mixed herbs and salt and stir well for one minute.
5. Then turn the heat to low and add the miso. Stir well.
6. Add the mint and the peas and stir well.
7. Finally, add 800 ml of water and bring the heat back up to medium.
8. Cook, stirring regularly until the soup is hot.
9. You can then blend your soup using a stick blender or mash with a potato masher for a chunkier texture. If your soup is too thick add a little extra water.
10. ENJOY!

CHICKEN NOODLE SOUP

Makes 4 servings

Chicken soup in a classic and always recommended when feeling under the weather. In this variation we have added our favourite, spinach, which gives an extra boost of iron and the essential vitamin K, along with A and C, to keep you strong and fighting fit for whatever life throws at you!

INGREDIENTS

- ⟩ 4 cloves garlic
- ⟩ 5 spring onions
- ⟩ 2 serving spoon frozen peas
- ⟩ 2 serving spoon frozen (or tinned) sweetcorn
- ⟩ 2 tsp lazy chilli
- ⟩ 2 pinches of salt
- ⟩ 1 handful spinach finely chopped, or two balls of frozen
- ⟩ 2 handfuls of roast chicken
- ⟩ 2 handfuls dried vermicelli noodles
- ⟩ 2 sachet miso soup
- ⟩ 2 dash fish sauce
- ⟩ 1 dstspn soy sauce
- ⟩ 1 dstspn of cooking oil
- ⟩ 800 ml water

METHOD

1. Peel the garlic and thinly slice, set to one side.
2. Trim the spring onions by chopping off the root ends (hairy bit) and any scraggly bits on the opposite end if you wish (although these are usually perfectly edible). Once trimmed, slice your spring onions all the way through the middle lengthways and then slice widthways to about 2-inch sized pieces. Set together with the garlic.
3. If you are using fresh spinach, roughly chop (or use scissors) and set to one side.
4. Heat your oil, on a medium heat, in a medium-sized saucepan.
5. Add the onions, garlic and salt and stir well for two minutes.
6. Then turn the heat to low and add the miso. Stir well.
7. Add the peas, sweetcorn, chilli and spinach, mix well, then add the soy and fish sauce.
8. Cook together stirring constantly for about 30 seconds, then add 800 ml of water and bring the heat back up to medium.
9. Add the chicken and noodles and stir for about two minutes, or until the noodles are soft.
10. ENJOY!

Minestrone soup

Makes 4 servings

This Italian classic is a meal in itself, packed full of fibre and all your essential vitamins!

Ingredients:

- 1 tin borlotti beans
- 1 tin tomatoes
- 1 carrot
- 2 celery sticks
- 2 handfuls spinach or 2 balls of frozen
- 1 red onion
- 3 cloves garlic
- 1 tsp mixed herbs
- 1 tsp dried basil
- 1 tsp smoked paprika
- 1 handful macaroni
- 2 pinches of salt
- 1 dstspn of cooking oil
- 800 ml water

Method:

1. Peel the carrot and top and tail (cut off each end). Next, finely dice the carrot and celery.
2. Peel and thinly slice or dice the onion and peel and grate the garlic.
3. Add the oil to a medium saucepan and place on your hob on a medium heat. Add the onion, garlic, carrot and celery.
4. Add the mixed herbs, dried basil and salt and give it all a good stir.
5. Cook for about 5 minutes, stirring regularly.
6. Open the beans, drain into a sieve and rinse under cold water; add these to your saucepan.
7. Add the tinned tomatoes, the water and the macaroni.
8. Using a wooden spoon, break down the tomatoes in the pan by pushing and stirring the ingredients.
9. Finally, add the spinach and paprika.
10. Give it all a good stir and turn your hob to a medium low heat.
11. Cook the soup, stirring regularly, for about ten minutes, or until the macaroni is soft.
12. ENJOY!

Tomato & sweet potato soup

Makes 4 servings

Sweet potatoes are rich in beta-carotene, which is converted by the body into the essential vitamin A, supporting eye health, skin health and your immune system. They are also a great source of fibre.

Ingredients

〉 1 onion
〉 4 cloves garlic
〉 1 medium sweet potato
〉 1 tsp paprika (optional)
〉 1 tsp mixed herbs
〉 2 pinches of salt
〉 1 tin tomatoes
〉 500 ml water
〉 1 dstspn cooking oil

Method

1. Peel the onion and garlic and roughly chop.
2. Peel the sweet potato and dice.
3. Add the oil to a medium saucepan and place on your hob on a medium heat.
4. Add the onions and garlic stir well for two minutes.
5. Add the mixed herbs and salt and give it all a really good stir.
6. Then add the sweet potato and cook for about five minutes, stirring regularly. Add a dash or two of water if it starts to stick (catch) on the pan.
7. Add the paprika (if using), mix well, then add the tomatoes and 500 ml of water.
8. Mix well and turn up the heat to bring to the boil. Then turn back to medium and cook, stirring regularly, for about ten minutes, or until the potato is soft.
9. You can then blend your soup using a stick blender or mash with a potato masher for a chunkier texture. If your soup is too thick add a little extra water.
10. ENJOY!

CARROT, CORIANDER, CARAWAY AND LENTIL SOUP
Makes 4 servings

Is it true that carrots help you see in the dark? Well, kind of. Carrots are full of vitamin A which is essential for good eye health. They are also a great source of fibre.

INGREDIENTS

> 4 cloves garlic
> 1 onion
> 4 medium carrots
> 1 tsp dried coriander
> 1 tsp caraway seeds
> 1 handful red split lentils
> 800 ml water
> 1 dstspn cooking oil
> 1 dstspn mixed seeds
> (optional)

METHOD

1. Peel the onion and garlic and roughly chop.
2. Peel the carrots, top and tail (cut off each end) and grate.
3. Add the oil to a medium saucepan and place on your hob on a medium heat.
4. Add the onions and garlic and stir well for two minutes.
5. Then add the carrot, coriander and caraway seeds. Cook, stirring regularly, for about two minutes.
6. Finally, add the lentils and salt and 800 ml of water. Cook on a medium to low heat, stirring regularly, for about ten minutes, or until the lentils are soft.
7. You can then blend your soup using a stick blender or mash with a potato masher for a chunkier texture. If your soup is too thick add a little extra water.
8. Finish with mixed seeds to add texture and crunch if desired.
9. **ENJOY!**

BURRITOS, QUESADILLA, FAJITAS & CHILLI

Burritos and quesadilla are fast becoming street food classics. Easy to make and highly versatile, these Mexican dishes are really filling and warming and can be filled with any combination of ingredients. A great way to use up fridge leftovers, for a quick lunch or dinner.

As well as knowing how to make them, assembling this street food so that it is easy to eat requires a bit of a knack, and we like to think we have perfected this! Here are step-by-step guides to creating a neat burrito wrap and a folded quesadilla.

How to assemble your burrito

1.

All your ingredients should be layered across the centre of the wrap.

6.

Then push the edge of the wrap to tuck under the filling ingredients.

2.

Start by folding in the sides.

7.

Finally tuck the ends in so that none of the filling can fall out.

3.

Holding the sides in steady, with your forefingers,

8.

Wrap in the foil

4.

Use your thumbs to fold over the long side.

9.

And carefully twist each end

5.

Press the wrap down using your forefingers.

10.

Now you are ready to carefully heat in your frying pan.

How to fold your quesadilla

1.
Cut a line from the centre of the wrap out to the edge.

2.
Take the outer edge of the cut and fold in towards the centre,

3.
So, one quarter of your quesadilla is folded.

4.
Then fold again, so that half of your quesadilla is folded.

5.
And again!

6.
Now you are ready to cook it.

Sweet potato & black bean burrito

Serves 1; Double up ingredients as necessary to enjoy with others.

Enjoy classic Mexican ingredients while filling up with fibre, five-a-day and flavour!

INGREDIENTS

- 2 wraps (wholemeal is best)
- 2 serving spoon roasted sweet potato
- 2 medium salad tomatoes
- 1 red onion
- 2 cloves garlic
- 2 tsp Cajun spice
- 1 tsp dried coriander
- ½ a lime (optional)
- 1 serving spoon (1/2 a tin) black beans.
- 2 handfuls of spinach
- About 20g cheddar cheese
- 1 handful white rice
- 1 handful brown rice
- Dash of hot sauce (if desired)
- 1 dstspn cooking oil
- 1 dstspn minted yogurt
- A handful of iceberg or cos lettuce (optional), to add texture.
- Tin foil

METHOD

1. Put the rice on to cook on a medium to high heat (it is more economical to boil the water in your kettle first than boil it on the hob). While the rice is cooking you can make your bean mix.
2. To prepare your bean mix, peel and dice the onion, peel and grate or finely chop the garlic and set these aside. Next, chop your tomatoes into small cubes (dice) and place in a mixing bowl. Using scissors, cut the spinach into thin strips and add to the tomatoes. Then in the same bowl add the beans, coriander and the juice and zest of the lime.
3. Grate your cheese and set aside separately.
4. Now you are ready to cook!
5. Start by frying off the onion and garlic on a medium heat with the Cajun spice; cook for about 2 minutes then add the bean mix. Cook on a medium heat for 8-10 minutes until the beans are soft and the liquid has evaporated.
6. Measure a square of foil which is slightly bigger than your wrap and place the wrap on top.
7. Layer up your burrito, like a rainbow, starting with the sweet potato (one serving spoon) which you can spread across the middle of the wrap, then add one spoon of your bean mix, and a dash of hot sauce (if you like it like that)!
8. Top with a sprinkle of cheese and 2 or 3 dessert spoons of rice. You can also add iceberg lettuce for texture and minted yogurt if you want.
9. FOLD (see *How to assemble your burrito* Pg. 40) – then wrap in the foil, twisting each end nice and tightly, like a sausage!
10. Finally, using a clean frying pan, on a low to medium heat, place your burrito in the pan, and "dry fry", turning each side to the heat for about 30 seconds, until all sides of the foil are warm - almost too hot to touch.
11. To eat (the important bit!), just peel back the foil and MUNCH!

CAJUN BLACK BEAN BURRITO

Serves 1; double up ingredients as necessary to enjoy with others.

Classic summer flavours for early evening sharing.

INGREDIENTS

> 1 serving spoon Cajun black bean mix (for recipe see Pg. 61)
> 1 handful spinach
> 2 dstspn coleslaw (for recipe see Pg. 61)
> 1 handful of rice (brown/white mix is best)
> 1 dash of hot sauce
> 1 small piece of cheddar cheese
> 1 large wrap (wholemeal is best)
> Tin foil

METHOD

1. Put the rice on to cook on a medium to high heat (it is more economical to boil the water in your kettle first than boil it on the hob).
2. While the rice is cooking grate the cheese.
3. Measure a square of foil which is slightly bigger than your wrap and place the wrap in top.
4. Once the rice is cooked, layer your ingredients across the wrap in a rainbow formation (see *How to assemble your burrito* Pg. 40), starting with the rice and finishing with the spinach. Roll the wrap and then wrap in the foil, twisting each end nice and tightly, like a sausage!
5. Finally, using a clean frying pan, on a low to medium heat, place your burrito in the pan, and "dry fry", turning each side to the heat for about 30 seconds, until all sides of the foil are warm - almost too hot to touch.
6. To eat (the important bit!) just peel back the foil and MUNCH!

FISHFINGER BURRITO

Serves 1; double up ingredients as necessary to enjoy with others.

Here we have combined a quintessentially British fish finger sandwich with the Mexican classic! The kids will love it too!

INGREDIENTS

> 3 fishfingers
> 1 handful of spinach
> 1 dstspn salsa (for recipe see Pg. 60)
> 2 dstspn coleslaw (for recipe see Pg. 61)
> 1 handful of rice (brown/ white mix is best)
> 1 dash of hot sauce
> 1 small piece of cheddar cheese
> 1 large wrap (wholemeal is best)
> Tin foil

METHOD

1. Put the rice on to cook on a medium to high heat (it is more economical to boil the water in your kettle first than boil it on the hob).
2. While the rice is cooking you can also cook the fishfingers under the grill and grate the cheese.
3. Measure a square of foil which is slightly bigger than your wrap and place the wrap on top.
4. When everything is cooked, layer your ingredients across the wrap in a rainbow formation (see *How to assemble your burrito* Pg. 40), starting with the rice and finishing with the spinach. Roll the wrap and then wrap in the foil, twisting each end nice and tightly, like a sausage!
5. Finally, using a clean frying pan, on a low to medium heat, place your burrito in the pan, and "dry fry", turning each side to the heat for about 30 seconds, until all sides of the foil are warm - almost too hot to touch.
6. To eat (the important bit!) just peel back the foil and MUNCH!

Fajitas burrito

Serves 1; double up ingredients as necessary to enjoy with others.

A great way to use up leftover fajitas mix!

Ingredients

> Chicken/ chickpea fajitas mix (leftovers or already cooked)

> 1 handful spinach

> 1 dstspn minted yogurt

> A handful of iceberg or cos lettuce (optional), to add texture.

> 1 handful of rice (brown/ white mix is best)

> 1 dash of hot sauce

> 1 small piece of cheddar cheese

> 1 large wrap (wholemeal is best)

> Tin foil

Method

1. Put the rice on to cook on a medium to high heat (it is more economical to boil the water in your kettle first than boil it on the hob).

2. While the rice is cooking you can grate the cheese, as well as heat your leftover fajitas mix (unless cooking from scratch, recipe on Pg. 55) in the microwave until piping hot.

3. Measure a square of foil which is slightly bigger than your wrap and place the wrap in top.

4. Once the rice is cooked, layer your ingredients across the wrap in a rainbow formation (see *How to assemble your burrito* Pg. 40), starting with the rice and finishing with the spinach. Roll the wrap and then wrap in the foil, twisting each end nice and tightly, like a sausage!

5. Finally, using a clean frying pan, on a low to medium heat, place your burrito in the pan, and "dry fry", turning each side to the heat for about 30 seconds, until all sides of the foil are warm - almost too hot to touch.

6. To eat (the important bit!) just peel back the foil and MUNCH!

Sweet potato & sweetcorn quesadilla

Serves 1; double up ingredients as necessary to enjoy with others.

Filling and satisfying – this quesadilla is comfort food at its best and full of fibre too.

Ingredients

> 1 wrap (wholemeal is best)
> 1 small piece of cheddar cheese
> 1 serving spoon roasted sweet potato (for recipe see Pg. 63)
> 2 dstspn frozen sweetcorn
> 1 handful of spinach
> 2 dstspn salsa (for recipe see Pg. 60)
> Dash of cooking oil

Method

1. Pop your sweetcorn in a mug of hot water for a few minutes to defrost and grate the cheese.
2. Place your wrap onto a chopping board, then, using a knife, cut from the centre of the wrap in a straight line to the outside edge of the wrap (see *How to fold your quesadilla* Pg. 41).
3. Place all the ingredients across the surface of the wrap.
4. Then, fold in half and half again.
5. Then heat a dash of oil in a frying pan on a medium heat. Carefully lift your quesadilla into the pan and fry gently, turning – using a fish slice - so that each side reaches a nice golden brown crispiness.
6. ENJOY!

BLACK BEAN & SPINACH QUESADILLA

Serves 1; double up ingredients as necessary to enjoy with others.

It's a great idea to combine food which are high in iron with food which are high in vitamin C, because vitamin C aids the absorption on iron into your body. So here we have combined black beans (which is high in iron) with spinach (which is high in vitamin C) to give your body a hearty, tasty energy boost.

INGREDIENTS

⟩ 1 wrap (wholemeal is best)
⟩ 1 small piece of cheddar cheese
⟩ 2 dstspn Cajun black bean mix (for recipe see Pg. 61)
⟩ 1 handful of spinach
⟩ Dash of cooking oil

METHOD

1. Grate the cheese.
2. Place your wrap onto a chopping board, then, using a knife, cut from the centre of the wrap in a straight line to the outside edge of the wrap (see *How to folding your quesadilla* Pg. 41).
3. Place all the ingredients across the surface of the wrap.
4. Then, fold in half and half again.
5. Then heat a dash of oil in a frying pan on a medium heat. Carefully lift your quesadilla into the pan and fry gently, turning - using a fish slice - so that each side reaches a nice golden brown crispiness.
6. ENJOY!

FAJITAS
Makes 4 portions

Fajitas are usually an absolute winner with all the family. Quick and easy to make, full of great nutrition and a great way to use up leftover bits and bobs in the fridge.

INGREDIENTS

> 4 wholemeal wraps
> 1 red pepper
> 1 yellow pepper
> 1 large red onion
> 2 handfuls of fresh spinach
> 2 chicken breasts (or you can use any other leftover chicken) or halloumi, or chickpeas!
> 8-10 cherry tomatoes
> Handful frozen sweetcorn
> Cheese if desired
> 1 tsp of mixed herbs
> 2 tsp of Cajun spice
> 1 dstspn cooking oil
> Mint and yogurt for the dip, if desired (for recipe see Pg. 60)

METHOD

1. Using a clean chopping board, thinly slice the chicken – or cut the halloumi into chunks. Wash your hands.
2. Now, using a different/clean board and knife, thinly slice the peppers and onion and set aside.
3. Cut the tomatoes in half and set aside.
4. Heat the oil in a medium-sized frying pan, on a medium heat. Add the mixed herbs, Cajun spice, peppers and onions, mix well and cook for about two minutes.
5. Then add the chicken or halloumi or chickpeas, stirring through the veg, and cook for a further five minutes, turning regularly.
6. Finally, add the tomatoes, spinach and sweetcorn; mix well and stir, cook for another two minutes.
7. When this is done, take your wraps, add a thin layer of yogurt dip (if using), and spread across the wrap, add the chicken/halloumi/chickpea & veg mix and a little grated cheese if desired, wrap, folding in the sides, and eat!
8. ENJOY!

SMOKY LENTIL, BLACK BEAN & SWEET POTATO CHILLI

Makes 4 portions

If you've never made your own chilli, now is the time to start. This recipe is easy, vegan, fibrous and as hot as you like! Enjoy!

INGREDIENTS

> 1 onion
> 4 cloves garlic
> 1 red pepper
> 1 medium sweet potato
> 1 tin of black beans
> 2 large handfuls or 3 small handfuls split red lentils
> 1 tsp cumin
> 1 tsp smoked paprika
> 1 dstsp lazy chilli for hot or ½ dstspn for medium hot
> 2 pinches of salt
> 1 dstspn cooking oil

METHOD

1. Peel and dice the onion. Peel and grate the garlic.
2. De-seed the pepper and thinly slice.
3. Peel the sweet potato and dice.
4. Heat the oil in a medium-sized frying pan, on a medium heat. Then add the garlic, onion, peppers and sweet potato to the pan, mix well so the veggies are coated in oil. Then add the cumin, paprika, chilli and salt, mix well and cook for two minutes.
5. Add a splash of water, mix well and cook for a further two minutes.
6. Then add the whole tin of black beans and two handfuls of red lentils.
7. Cook until the lentils and sweet potato are soft, adding more water through the cooking process if necessary.
8. Serve with a white and brown rice mix, pitta or couscous.
9. ENJOY!

BURRITO EXTRAS

These are accompaniments to your burrito that turn a snack into a complete meal.

 PG. 60   Tomato salsa

 PG. 60   Minted yogurt

 PG. 61   Coleslaw

 PG. 61   Cajun black bean

 PG. 63   Roasted sweet potato

 Easy-Read recipe pg 145

Tomato salsa

Ingredients

> 4 salad tomatoes
> ½ onion
> 2 cloves garlic
> 1 lime, zest and juice
> 1 tsp dried coriander

Method

1. Dice the tomatoes.
2. Peel and finely dice the onion.
3. Peel the garlic and finely chop.
4. Zest the lime and squeeze the juice.
5. Add all this to a bowl with the coriander and mix well.
6. If possible, leave for an hour or more so that the ingredients break down a little bit.
7. ENJOY!

Minted yogurt

Ingredients

> 500ml plain yogurt
> 3 or 4 sprigs of mint

Method

1. Take the leaves of mint from their stalks and finely chop.
2. Mix in a bowl with the yogurt.
3. ENJOY!

👁 Easy-Read recipe pg 138

COLESLAW

INGREDIENTS

- ❭ 1 red onion
- ❭ ¼ red cabbage
- ❭ 2 medium carrots
- ❭ 1 dstspn mayonnaise
- ❭ 1 dstspn plain yogurt

METHOD

1. Thinly slice the red cabbage.
2. Peel the onion and finely slice.
3. Peel, top and tail the carrots and grate.
4. Mix everything together in bowl with the yogurt and mayonnaise.
5. ENJOY!

👁 Easy-Read recipe pg 140

CAJUN BLACK BEAN

INGREDIENTS

- ❭ 1 onion
- ❭ 2 tsp Cajun spice
- ❭ 1 tin of tomatoes
- ❭ 1 tin of black beans
- ❭ 2 cloves garlic
- ❭ 1 dstspn cooking oil

METHOD

1. Peel the onion and finely dice.
2. Peel the garlic and finely chop or grate.
3. Heat the oil in a medium saucepan on a medium heat then add the garlic and onion and mix well. Cook for two minutes, stirring regularly.
4. Then add the black beans and the Cajun spice, mix well and cook for two minutes, stirring regularly.
5. Finally add the tomatoes, mix well. Turn the heat to low and cook for about ten minutes or until the beans are soft and there is minimal liquid left from the tomatoes.
6. Mash roughly with a fork – not completely as you want to keep some of the texture.
7. ENJOY!

Roasted sweet potato

Ingredients

> 2 medium sweet potatoes
> 1 dstspn cooking oil
> 1 pinch of salt

Method

1. Peel the sweet potato and dice.
2. Place in a medium-sized baking dish and toss with the oil and salt until completely covered.
3. Cook in the oven for 20-30 minutes or until soft.
4. ENJOY!

CURRIES

Curry represents everything that is great about multicultural Britain! It's such a wonderfully versatile concept, fully adaptable to your tastes, accessible and easy to cook at home and a great way to use up odds and ends in the fridge. What's not to love!

CHICKEN CURRY
Makes 4 portions

It's a classic! In this curry, for simplicity we use a curry paste. As you continue through this section you will learn how easy it is to make your own. Homemade curries are a great way to use up what's in the fridge and are really good for you.

INGREDIENTS

> 1 red pepper
> 1 yellow pepper
> 1 green pepper
> 1 onion
> 4 cloves garlic
> 1 tin of tomatoes
> 1 dstspn of hot curry paste (or strength of paste to taste)
> 1 tsp garam masala
> 1 tsp cumin
> 2 tsp dried coriander leaf
> 2-3 handfuls of leftover roast chicken or 2 chicken breasts (if cooking from scratch)
> 2 serving spoons peas
> 1 dstspn oil
> Tap water

METHOD

1. Peel the onion and large dice.
2. Peel the garlic and finely chop or grate.
3. Next, de-seed the peppers and roughly large dice.
4. If you are using fresh (raw) chicken, you can prepare that by chopping it into thin strips. Remember to wash your hands after handling this and wash down your chopping board.
5. Heat the oil in a medium-sized frying pan on a medium heat. Add the spices and coriander and gently mix with a wooden spoon, to make a paste.
6. If you are using fresh chicken, first add this to the pan and cook, turning regularly, for about three minutes (if you are using leftover chicken, you can add it later in the recipe).
7. Add the onion and garlic and mix well. Cook for about two minutes,
8. Then add the peppers and cook for a further two minutes, mixing well and stirring regularly.
9. Add about 1/3 of a mug of water (about 100ml), stir, and cook for about five minutes.
10. Add the curry paste and mix well, then add the tin of tomatoes.
11. Now, using a masher or the back of a fork, break down the tomatoes and stir through the other ingredients, cook for five minutes, or until the peppers are soft but have a "bite."
12. Finally, add the peas and leftover chicken and cook for a further two or three minutes.
13. Serve with a white and brown rice mix, naan bread or pitta bread or couscous.
14. ENJOY!

Sweet potato curry

Makes 4 portions

Sweet potatoes are rich in beta-carotene, which is converted by the body into the essential vitamin A, supporting eye health, skin health and your immune system. They are also a great source of fibre.

Ingredients

- 1 tin of tomatoes
- 1 onion
- 2 handfuls of spinach, or two balls of frozen
- 4 cloves garlic
- 2 serving spoons of frozen peas
- 2 medium sweet potatoes
- 1 tsp cumin powder
- 1 tsp garam masala
- 2 dstspn medium-hot curry powder
- 4 tsp dried coriander leaf
- 1 dstspn cooking oil

Method

1. Peel and dice your potatoes, peel and dice the onion and peel and grate the garlic.
2. Chop the spinach into thin strips.
3. Heat the oil in a medium-sized frying pan on a medium heat. Add the spices, curry powder and coriander and gently mix with a wooden spoon, to make a paste.
4. Add the garlic and onion, mix well, then add the sweet potato. Cook, stirring regularly for about two minutes.
5. Add the tinned tomatoes and then fill the tin again with water – to get all the lovely juice – and add this too. Turn the heat to medium high, bring to the boil. Turn the heat back to medium and cook for about 15 minutes, or until the potatoes are soft, adding more water if necessary (enough to keep a thick sauce consistency).
6. Finally, add the peas and spinach and stir through the curry until everything is hot.
7. Serve with a white and brown rice mix, naan bread or pitta bread or couscous.
8. ENJOY!

BEETROOT CURRY

Makes 4 portions

Ahh, the super beet! Beetroot is a great source of fibre, iron and vitamin C. They are easy to grow and will sit happily in the ground, long into the autumn. When in season they can be found quite cheaply at farmers' markets and will freeze well (cook and freeze in batches).

INGREDIENTS

-) 4 medium beetroot
-) 1 red pepper
-) 1 yellow pepper
-) 1 green pepper
-) 1 onion
-) 4 cloves garlic
-) 1 tsp lazy chilli
-) 1 tin of tomatoes
-) 1 dstspn medium or hot curry paste
-) 1 tsp caraway seeds
-) 1 tsp cumin
-) 2 tsp coriander leaf
-) 1 dstspn cooking oil

METHOD

1. Peel and dice the beetroot and set aside – be warned, the juice gets everywhere (but don't worry, it doesn't stain!) You may also want to wear gloves.

2. De-seed and roughly large dice the peppers. I think it looks nice if the peppers are all slightly different shapes and sizes (no rules here!).

3. Peel and thinly slice the onion; peel and grate the garlic.

4. Heat the oil in a medium-sized frying pan on a medium heat. Add the spices, caraway seeds and coriander and gently mix with a wooden spoon, to make a paste.

5. Add the garlic and onion, mix well, then add the peppers. Cook, stirring regularly for about two minutes.

6. Add your beetroot and the lazy chilli. Mix well. Add the tinned tomatoes and then fill the tin again with water – to get all the lovely juice – and add this too. Turn the heat to medium high, bring to the boil. Turn the heat back to medium and cook for about 15 minutes, or until the beetroot is soft, adding more water if necessary (enough to keep a thick sauce consistency).

7. Serve with a white and brown rice mix, naan bread or pitta bread or couscous.

8. ENJOY!

Harrison's Curry
Makes 4 portions

This recipe was designed for three-year-old Harrison. Harrison's mum was worried about coming to Grub Club because of her children's specific dietary requirements related to certain allergies, but she was soon at ease. Harrison's family have learnt loads of new recipes and ideas for healthy, balanced vegan meals which also accommodate their allergies.

Ingredients

> 1 tsp turmeric powder
> 1 dstspn med hot tandoori or curry powder
> 1 tsp garam masala
> 1 tsp cumin
> 2 pinches of salt
> 2 dstspn milled seeds
> 1 dstspn cooking oil
> 1 onion
> 6 cloves garlic
> ½ a red pepper
> ½ a green pepper
> ½ a yellow pepper
> A thumb-sized piece of ginger
> 1 tin of chickpeas
> 1 tin of coconut milk
> 2 serving spoon frozen or tinned sweetcorn
> 1 lime – juice and zest
> 1 tsp mango chutney or honey (optional)

Method

1. Peel and thinly slice the onion; peel and grate the garlic.
2. Peel and grate the ginger – don't worry if it doesn't grate well, it will cook well into the sauce regardless. Top tip – the easiest way to peel ginger is with a teaspoon – try it! This is easy to do – just hold the piece of ginger firmly and use the curved end of a teaspoon as a type of peeler to remove the skin. Far less waste than cutting the skin off with a knife!
3. De-seed and roughly large dice the peppers. I think it looks nice if the peppers are all slightly different shapes and sizes (no rules here!).
4. Heat the oil in a medium-sized frying pan on a medium heat. Add the spices and curry powder and gently mix with a wooden spoon, to make a paste.
5. Next add the garlic, ginger and onion, mix well, then add the peppers. Cook for about 30 seconds, then add one mug of water (about 350ml) and cook for another two minutes, stirring regularly.
6. Drain the chickpeas using a sieve and add to the pan, along with the lime juice and zest, the milled seeds, and two pinches of salt.
7. Open the coconut milk and give it a stir (the fats tend to separate). Now add the coconut milk to your sauce. Give it all a good stir and cook for about 15-20 minutes or until the sauce has thickened.
8. Finally, add a little mango chutney or honey to sweeten and taste.
9. Serve with a white and brown rice mix, naan bread or pitta bread or couscous.
10. ENJOY!

Cauliflower & coconut milk curry

Makes 4 portions

Cauliflowers are generally quite big, and they certainly go a long way! So, it is no wonder that the cauliflower is one of those vegetables that get left in the fridge and no one knows what to do with it! This is a tasty way to use it up and freezes well.

Ingredients

> 1 tsp turmeric powder
> 1 dstspn med hot tandoori or curry powder
> 1 tsp garam masala
> 1 tsp cumin
> 2 pinches of salt
> 1 dstspn cooking oil
> 1 onion
> 4 cloves garlic
> ½ a cauliflower
> A thumb-sized piece of ginger
> 4 balls of frozen spinach
> 1 tin of coconut milk
> 1 handful of red split lentils

Method

1. Peel and thinly slice the onion; peel and grate the garlic.
2. Peel and grate the ginger – don't worry if it doesn't grate well, it will cook well into the sauce regardless.
3. Roughly chop the cauliflower (stalks, leaves and all) into bite sized pieces.
4. Now, heat the oil in a medium-sized frying pan on a medium heat. Add the spices and curry powder and gently mix with a wooden spoon, to make a paste.
5. Next add the garlic, ginger and onion, mix well, then add the cauliflower. Cook for about 30 seconds.
6. Open the coconut milk and give it a stir (the fats tend to separate). Now add the coconut milk to your pan. Give it all a good stir and cook for about ten minutes.
7. Add the spinach to the sauce and cook for a further five minutes, gently breaking it down with a fork as it starts to defrost.
8. Cook until your sauce has thickened, and the cauliflower and lentils are soft.
9. Serve with a white and brown rice mix, naan bread or pitta bread or couscous.
10. ENJOY!

WORKSHOPS

We run after-school clubs called Grub Clubs for families with children; Munch Lunch Club for adults; online courses which help people become better orientated in their own kitchens; and holiday cooking workshops (kids only).

Our format is simple: we provide recipes, ingredients and everybody cooks their own food. We all sit down and eat together and leftovers are taken home to enjoy at a later date.

Our ethos is sustainable nutrition. We help people make flexible eating changes with a strong emphasis on high fibre, fruit and veg and low to no levels of meat.

Beyond this, our workshops provide a safe and sociable environment where people can learn all about cooking and healthy eating as well as experience the benefits of eating together, being part of a community, and the incredible impact this has on general wellbeing.

For more info head to our website www.munchcic.co.uk

PASTA AND RISOTTO

Everyone loves Italian food!

As with curries, pasta and risotto dishes can be made with pretty much anything and are a great way to save wasting random fridge finds. In our pasta section we've added some 'ball' recipes, as shop produced meat/fish/vegan balls can be really high in salt and added flavours. This way you can experiment with making your own - it's fun to do with the kids as well.

Risottos should be full of love and ours certainly are. The beetroot risotto is my favourite autumn dish, it's so easy and tastes delicious!

Base tomato sauce

Makes 4-6 portions - can double up as tomato soup (and regularly does in our house)!

Shop-bought pasta sauce is high in salt and added sugars. By making your own you are in control of what goes in. This sauce can be made in large batches and frozen in portions. It's a great base for soups, stews, curries, pastas and pizza. We use carrots in our tomato sauce as a great way to sneak in extra veggies and also add sweetness.

Ingredients

- 2 medium carrots
- 1 onion
- 4 cloves garlic
- 2 tins of tomatoes
- 2 tsp mixed herbs
- 2 pinches of salt
- 1 dstspn honey or 1 tsp agave if vegan
- 1 dstspn cooking oil

Method

1. Peel and dice the onion and peel and grate the garlic.
2. Peel the carrots, top and tail (cut off each end) and grate.
3. Add the oil to a medium/large saucepan and place on your hob on a medium heat.
4. Add the salt and mixed herbs, give it a good stir, then immediately add the onions and garlic and stir well for two minutes.
5. Then add the carrot and cook, stirring regularly, for about two minutes.
6. Add the tomatoes. Half fill each tomato tin again with water to rinse out all the lovely juices that get stuck in the tin and add to your sauce. Mix well.
7. Finally add the honey/agave and mix well for 30 seconds.
8. You can then blend your sauce using a stick blender or mash with a potato masher for a chunkier texture. If your sauce is too thick add a little extra water.
9. ENJOY!

Arrabiata pasta
Makes 2 portions

An Italian classic! Make as hot as you like!

Ingredients

> 6 cloves garlic
> 1 onion
> 2 tsp dried basil
> 2 pinches of salt
> 3 dstspn lazy chilli (or 2 fresh chillies, finely diced)
> 1 tsp honey or agave if vegan
> 1 dstspn tomato puree (optional)
> 1 tin of tomatoes
> Parmesan (optional)
> 1 handful of dry pasta per portion
> 1 dstspn cooking oil

Method

1. Peel and dice the onion and peel and grate the garlic.
2. Add the oil to a medium/large saucepan and place on your hob on a medium heat.
3. Add the salt and basil, give it a good stir, then immediately add the onions and garlic and stir well for two minutes.
4. Add the chilli and tomato puree, cook, stirring regularly, for about one minute.
5. Add the tomatoes. Quarter fill the tomato tin again with water to rinse out all the lovely juices that get stuck in the tin and add to your sauce. Mix well.
6. Finally add the honey/agave and mix well for 30 seconds.
7. Mash with a potato masher to break down the tomatoes a little but retain a chunky texture. If your sauce is too thick add a little extra water.
8. Cook the pasta and add a little parmesan if desired.
9. ENJOY!

YUMMY SCRUMMY VIBRANT TUNA PASTA
Makes 4 portions

This dish screams summer! Full of colour and flavour, it's an easy peasy family favourite.

INGREDIENTS

> 1 onion
> 4 cloves garlic
> 1 red pepper
> 1 yellow pepper
> 2 serving spoons of frozen sweetcorn
> 2 handfuls of fresh spinach or 2 balls of frozen
> Cherry tomatoes (optional)
> 1 dstspn cooking oil
> 2 tins of tuna (in spring water, if possible)
> 1 tin of tomatoes
> 2 tsp mixed herbs
> 1 pinch of salt

METHOD

1. Peel the onion and dice or thinly slice; peel and grate the garlic.
2. De-seed the peppers and roughly dice or thinly slice (whichever you prefer).
3. Heat the oil in a medium frying pan on a medium heat.
4. Add the garlic and onions, mixed herbs and salt. Stir and cook for about a minute; then add the peppers. Cook for three minutes, stirring regularly.
5. Add the tinned tomatoes. Half fill the tomato tin again with water to rinse out all the lovely juices that get stuck in the tin and add to your sauce. Mix well.
6. Finally, add the tuna, sweetcorn and spinach and cook for about five minutes, breaking down the spinach as it defrosts, with the back of a fork.
7. Serve with pasta of your choice.
8. ENJOY!

TUNA BALLS
Makes about 20 balls

Tuna contains healthy omega-3 and essential fatty acids. It is also high in B vitamins, iron and proteins. Tuna is often the only fish that children will eat, and so this is a great way to get the kids involved in cooking as it's fun to make the mix and roll the balls. Make the batch, cook, and freeze leftovers. This recipe is gluten and egg free.

INGREDIENTS

⟩ 3 tins tuna in oil
⟩ 3 dstspn milled seeds
⟩ 1 handful of fresh spinach
⟩ 2 tsp dried basil
⟩ ½ lemon, juice and zest
⟩ 1 red pepper
⟩ 1 tsp hot paprika
⟩ A pinch of salt

METHOD

1. De-seed the pepper and very finely dice.
2. Very finely chop the spinach.
3. Drain the tuna but keep the oil as you can use this for cooking.
4. Juice and zest the lemon.
5. Put all your ingredients into a mixing bowl (apart from the tuna oil).
6. Mix all the ingredients until they start to stick together. If they are not sticking very well just add a very small amount of the tuna oil.
7. Then roll your balls. To do this it helps to have wet hands! Roll each ball to about the size of a small golf ball.
8. Cook the tuna balls either on a greased baking tray in the oven - for about 10 minutes – or, using the oil from the tuna tins, you can pan fry in batches, gently on a medium heat, turning regularly until they are hot all the way through. Pan frying will be more time-consuming and require more attention, plus, depending on how much oil you use, it can be messy and unhealthy! The oven is preferable, as the time difference in cooking evens out the cost in energy.
9. Once your balls are ready, serve with pasta and a homemade tomato sauce (see recipe Pg. 81)
10. ENJOY!

Spicy ricey bean balls

Makes about 20

Vegan, gluten free, egg free, rammed full of fibre and totally delicious! These balls are really filling! Cook the batch and freeze the leftovers.

Ingredients

⟩ 1 onion

⟩ 4 cloves garlic

⟩ 8 closed cup or chestnut mushrooms

⟩ 1 tin of black beans

⟩ 1 handful brown rice cooked until really soft

⟩ 3 dstspn milled seeds

⟩ 1 tsp hot paprika

⟩ 1 tsp mixed herbs

⟩ A pinch of salt

⟩ 1 dstspn cooking oil

Method

1. Peel and finely dice the onion, peel and finely chop the garlic, peel and finely chop the mushrooms.

2. Drain the black beans. If you have a food processor, use this to break down the beans, being careful to retain a bit of texture. If you do not have a processor, place the beans in a mixing bowl and break them down by firmly pressing with the back of a fork or your fingers.

3. When the beans are broken down, add all your ingredients to a mixing bowl (apart from the oil).

4. Mix all the ingredients until they start to stick together. If they are not sticking very well just add a very small amount of oil.

5. Then roll your balls. To do this it helps to have wet hands! Roll each ball to about the size of a small golf ball.

6. Cook the bean balls either on a greased baking tray in the oven - for about 10 minutes – or, using some oil, you can pan fry in batches, gently on a medium heat, turning regularly until they are hot all the way through. Pan frying will be more time-consuming and require more attention, plus, depending on how much oil you use, it can be messy and unhealthy! The oven is preferable, as the time difference in cooking evens out the cost in energy.

7. Once your balls are ready, serve with pasta and a homemade tomato sauce (see recipe Pg. 81)

8. ENJOY!

Turkey balls

Makes about 20

Turkey is a cheaper, more environmentally friendly alternative to beef. It is also a great lean source of protein.

Ingredients

> 1 onion
> 3 dstspn milled seeds
> 2 tsp mixed herbs
> 2 tsp dried basil
> 2 pinches of salt
> 750g turkey mince

Method

1. Peel and finely dice the onion.
2. Put all the ingredients into a bowl and mix until they start to stick together.
3. Then roll your balls. To do this it helps to have wet hands! Roll each ball to about the size of a small golf ball.
4. Cook the turkey balls either on a greased baking tray in the oven - for about 10 minutes – or, using some oil, you can pan fry in batches, gently on a medium heat, turning regularly until they are cooked all the way through. Pan frying will be more time consuming and require more attention, plus, depending on how much oil you use, it can be messy and unhealthy! The oven is preferable, as the time difference in cooking evens out the cost in energy.
5. Once your balls are ready, serve with pasta and a homemade tomato sauce (see recipe Pg. 81)
6. ENJOY!

WILD GARLIC

Wild garlic is a wonderful (free!) ingredient to use in your cooking and can be found in abundance in woodland and sometimes even on suburban street corners! Take care, as it is similar in appearance to other inedible forest plants. However, you can't mistake it because of its wafting aroma (of garlic, obviously) and beautiful white flowers! Wild garlic has become trendy in recent years and there is always a buzz of excitement around chef types when the first leaves start to flourish in mid-late spring. It's great in pesto, salads and sauces.

Be mindful and considerate when you forage. It has a strong flavour, so you really don't need to go crazy. Just take what you need and if you come across an already rather depleted patch try to find somewhere else, where it lies in abundance, before picking your leaves.

No-nut wild garlic and watercress pesto

This makes enough for 4 servings of pasta.

You will need a blender for this recipe.

INGREDIENTS

〉 A thumb-sized piece of parmesan
〉 1 clove garlic
〉 100ml olive oil
〉 1 handful wild garlic
〉 1 handful watercress
〉 ½ a lemon
〉 1 pinch of salt
〉 2 dstspn mixed seeds

METHOD

1. Using scissors, roughly chop your wild garlic and watercress into the blender bowl.
2. Peel the garlic clove and grate that and the parmesan into the bowl. Juice the lemon and add this to the other ingredients, then zest the lemon into the bowl as well. Add the seeds, salt and oil.
3. Blitz the ingredients together until you have a smooth pesto paste. You may need to stop occasionally to push any escaped ingredients back down inside to the bottom of the bowl!
4. Eat with pasta – plain, veggie or tuna – or toss through a salad.
5. ENJOY!

Summer veggies with wild garlic pasta
Makes 4 portions

Pretty much all the fresh ingredients here can be grown in the garden, making it really sustainable and super healthy. It can easily be made vegan and tastes great.

Ingredients

> 2 handfuls of wild garlic
> 2 handfuls of spinach
> 1 handful of fresh mint (optional)
> 1 handful of fresh basil (optional)
> 3 salad tomatoes
> ½ a lemon
> ½ a courgette
> 2 serving spoons frozen peas
> 1 dstspn cooking oil
> 2 tsp caraway seeds
> A pinch of salt
> A thumb-sized piece of parmesan (optional)
> 1 handful of dry pasta per portion

Method

1. Pre-cook your pasta, cool and set aside.
2. If you have foraged the wild garlic, wash it thoroughly, and rinse the other veg too.
3. Squeeze the lemon and set the juice aside.
4. Then prepare all your vegetables in the same mixing bowl:
5. Rough chop (or use scissors) the spinach, basil, mint and wild garlic. Next, dice the tomatoes, remembering to catch the juice! Zest the lemon. Peel the courgette into ribbons (by running a peeler down each side as you would if you were peeling a carrot), chopping any remaining that can't be ribboned. Add the peas, caraway seeds and salt and mix well.
6. Heat the oil in a large frying pan on a medium heat. Add the contents of your mixing bowl and stir well, cook for about three minutes, then add the lemon juice and cook for another minute or so, stirring constantly.
7. Finally, quickly add the pasta and grate the parmesan straight into the pan, mix well for about 30 seconds then serve.
8. ENJOY!

Spring veg risotto

Makes 4-6 portions

This essential immune-boosting risotto uses all the greens, giving you a hit of vitamins K and C, keeping your blood and heart healthy. It tastes clean, fresh and delicious.

Ingredients

⟩ 1 onion
⟩ 4 cloves garlic
⟩ 4 spring onions
⟩ 2 handfuls of fresh spinach or 2 balls of frozen
⟩ 2 tsp mixed herbs
⟩ 1 handful mint
⟩ 2 serving spoons frozen peas
⟩ 1 handful of wild garlic
⟩ 1 handful of fresh rocket
⟩ 1 sachet miso soup
⟩ 1 pinch of salt
⟩ 1 dstspn cooking oil
⟩ 1 lemon, juice and zest
⟩ 2 handfuls arborio/risotto rice
⟩ Parmesan (optional)
⟩ 1 litre water

Method

1. Peel and small dice the onion; peel and grate the garlic.
2. Trim the spring onions by chopping off the root ends (hairy bit) and any scraggly bits on the opposite end if you wish (although these are usually perfectly edible). Once trimmed, slice your spring onions on a slant so that you have biggish oval-shaped discs.
3. If you are using fresh spinach, roughly chop (or use scissors) and set to one side. If you are using frozen spinach, pop it in a mug of hot water to defrost and separate with a fork (this takes about two minutes).
4. Juice and zest the lemon (using the smallest blade on the grater).
5. Thoroughly wash and then roughly chop (or use scissors) the wild garlic.
6. Boil 800 ml water in your kettle, put it in a jug or bowl, then add 200ml cold water. Add the miso soup paste and mix well.
7. Heat the oil in a medium-sized frying pan on a medium heat. Add the garlic and onion, mixed herbs and salt and mix well. Cook, stirring regularly for about two minutes.
8. Add the rice and mix well.
9. Add one ladle (or cup) of this water to the rice.
10. Cook on a medium to low heat until the water has all disappeared into the rice, then add another ladle/mug of water.
11. Repeat this process until the rice is soft, but with a bite.
12. Finally - near the end of the rice-cooking process – add the spinach, peas, lemon juice and zest, wild garlic, mint and rocket, stirring through the rice until the greens have wilted.
13. Serve with parmesan if desired.
14. ENJOY!

Summer mackerel risotto
Makes 4-6 portions

Mackerel is a great source of protein, omega-3 and B vitamins, which are important for brain health and for converting food to energy in our bodies. Ready-cooked mackerel fillets can often be found in the reduced section in the supermarket, they keep well in the fridge and freeze well too. Be careful of pin bones in your fillets!

Ingredients

> 3 ready-cooked mackerel fillets.
> 4 cloves garlic
> 1 red onion
> 4 spring onions
> 1 medium courgette
> 2 serving spoons peas
> 1 lemon juice and zest
> 1 sachet miso soup
> 2 pinches of salt
> 1 dstspn cooking oil
> 3 small handfuls or 2 large handfuls arborio/risotto rice
> Parmesan (optional)
> 2 handfuls of fresh spinach or 2 balls of frozen
> A dash of fish sauce
> 2 tsp Cajun spice
> 1 tsp of caraway seeds
> 1 tsp dried basil
> 1 litre water

Method

1. Zest and juice the lemon.
2. Peel and small dice the onion; peel and grate the garlic.
3. Trim the spring onions by chopping off the root ends (hairy bit) and any scraggly bits on the opposite end if you wish (although these are usually perfectly edible). Once trimmed, slice your spring onions on a slant so that you have biggish oval-shaped discs.
4. If you are using fresh spinach, roughly chop (or use scissors) and set to one side. if you are using frozen spinach, pop it in a mug of hot water to defrost and separate with a fork (this takes about two minutes).
5. Prepare your courgette by topping and tailing and making ribbons using a peeler, then chop the ribbons so they are bite-sized. Chop any remaining un-ribboned courgette up small.
6. Remove the silver skin from the mackerel fillets, then shred the mackerel by ripping it apart with your hands.
7. Make the miso 'stock.' Boil 800 ml water in your kettle, put it in a jug or bowl then add 200ml cold water. Add the miso soup paste and mix well.
8. Heat the oil in a medium-sized frying pan on a medium heat. Add the garlic and red onion, basil, salt, Cajun spice mixed herbs and caraway and mix well. Cook, stirring regularly for about two minutes.
9. Add the spring onion, courgette, lemon juice and rice, mix well and cook for about two minutes.
10. Add one ladle (or cup) of the miso stock water to the rice.
11. Cook on a medium to low heat until the water has all disappeared into the rice, then add another ladle/mug of water.
12. Repeat this process until the rice is soft, but with a bite.
13. Finally - near the end of the rice-cooking process – add the spinach, peas, lemon zest, fish sauce and shredded mackerel fillets.
14. Serve with parmesan if desired.
15. ENJOY!

Autumn beetroot risotto

Makes 4-6 portions

Caraway is a plant native to western Asia. It is high in fibre, important trace minerals and iron. Beetroot is a great source of fibre, iron and vitamin C. They are easy to grow and will sit happily in the ground, long into the autumn. When in season they can be found quite cheaply at farmers' markets and will freeze well (cook and freeze in batches).

Ingredients

> 1 onion
>
> 4 cloves garlic
>
> 3 medium beetroot
>
> 2 tsp caraway seeds
>
> 1 tsp mixed herbs
>
> 1 sachet miso soup
>
> 1 pinch of salt
>
> 1 dstspn cooking oil
>
> 2 handfuls arborio/risotto rice
>
> Parmesan (optional)
>
> 1 litre water

Method

1. Peel and dice the beetroot and set aside – be warned, the juice gets everywhere (but don't worry, it doesn't stain!) You may also want to wear gloves.
2. Peel and small dice the onion; peel and grate the garlic.
3. Heat the oil in a medium-sized frying pan on a medium heat. Add the garlic and onion, salt, mixed herbs and caraway and mix well. Cook, stirring regularly for about two minutes.
4. Add the rice, mix well and cook for about two minutes, then add the beetroot and mix well.
5. Boil 800 ml water in your kettle, put it in a jug or bowl then add 200ml cold water. Add the miso soup paste and mix well.
6. Add one ladle (or cup) of this water to the rice.
7. Cook on a medium to low heat until the water has all disappeared into the rice, then add another ladle/mug of water.
8. Repeat this process until the rice is soft – with a bite – and the beetroot is soft too.
9. Serve with parmesan if desired.
10. ENJOY!

JAMBALAYA!
Makes 4 portions

This dish is really tasty, and you can chuck anything in it so it's a great way to use up fridge odds and ends. I've chosen to include mackerel, as it is high in omega 3 – essential for hair, skin and cell reproduction. It's cheap, stretches well, keeps well in the fridge and freezes well too!

INGREDIENTS

> 1 tin chopped tomatoes
> 1 onion
> 4 cloves garlic
> ½ a red pepper
> Mixed frozen veg – I use peas, sweetcorn and green beans
> 2 handfuls brown rice
> 1 handful white rice
> 1 dstspn mixed seeds
> ½ tin tap water (plus more if needed)
> 1 dstspn cooking oil
> 1 pinch of salt
> 2 tsp mixed herbs
> 2 tsp smoked paprika
> 1 sachet miso soup
> 1 tsp fish sauce
> Pre-cooked chicken thighs x 2
> 1 ready-cooked mackerel fillet

METHOD

1. Peel and dice the onion, peel and grate or finely chop the garlic, de-seed and roughly chop the pepper.

2. Boil 800 ml water in your kettle, put it in a jug or bowl then add 200ml cold water. Add the miso soup paste and mix well.

3. Now, heat the oil in a medium sized frying pan, on a medium heat. Add the onion and garlic and cook, stirring regularly, for about one minute. Then add the rice, seeds, mixed herbs, salt, paprika and fish sauce – stir well and cook for two minutes.

4. Then add the tomatoes, peppers and one ladle of miso water; bring to the boil, then turn to a medium low heat and simmer, stirring occasionally, until the water has all disappeared into the rice, then add another ladle/mug of water.

5. Repeat this process until the rice is soft, with a bite, and you have a risotto consistency.

6. Finally - near the end of the rice cooking process - add all the frozen veg and any meat/ fish that you are including. Mix in thoroughly and cook through until hot.

7. ENJOY!

STIR FRIES

Another fine example of stolen cuisine! The stir fry technique originates in China but has certainly become a common staple across households in the UK.

Yet another perfect way to use up fresh ingredients – the recipes in this section give you some base ideas of how to successfully combine flavours and spices – you can swap and change vegetables as you wish.

Super greens stir fry

Makes 4-6 portions

Rammed full of iron, antioxidant and vitamins A and K! This is a perfect mid-week meal to get you through to Friday!

Ingredients

- 1 courgette – ribbons
- Half a head of broccoli (or around 8 florets)
- 2 handfuls fresh spinach
- 6 kale leaves/spring greens/ savoy cabbage
- 3 spring onions
- 1 serving spoon frozen peas
- 3 cloves garlic
- 1 handful of salted peanuts - halved
- 1 handful of mixed seeds
- 2 nests of vermicelli noodles
- 1 tsp turmeric
- 1 dstspn cooking oil
- 1 dstspn low-salt soy sauce
- 1 sachet miso soup

Method

1. Prepare your vegetables - you can put them all in the same bowl before cooking as they will all be cooked together.
2. Peel the garlic and thinly slice.
3. Trim the spring onions by chopping off the root ends (hairy bit) and any scraggly bits on the opposite end if you wish (although these are usually perfectly edible). Once trimmed slice your spring onions on a slant so that you have biggish oval-shaped discs.
4. Roughly chop (or use scissors) the spinach.
5. De-stalk your greens (see Pg. 14) and slice thinly into strips, and thinly slice the broccoli florets, width ways so they still have the floret shape (like little flat trees!).
6. Prepare your courgette by topping and tailing and making ribbons using a peeler.
7. Heat your oil in a large frying pan, on a medium heat. Add the contents of your mixing bowl and stir well, cook for about three minutes, then add the soy and the miso paste, and cook for another five or so, stirring constantly, until the broccoli is soft but still has a bite. Then take the pan off the heat.
8. Now place the noodles in a saucepan and boil enough water (using a kettle as this is more economical) to cover them. Once boiled, add the water to the pan, along with the turmeric and cook on a medium heat for about 30-60 seconds.
9. Drain the noodles over the sink with a sieve then add to your stir fry.
10. Bring the stir fry back to the heat and finally add the peanuts, the peas and the mixed seeds. Toss everything together so that it is all mixed well and fully heated through.
11. ENJOY!

Chow Mein

Makes 4 portions

The perfect 'fake-away'! This recipe uses chicken, but an excellent veggie alternative is to use chickpeas.

Ingredients

> 2 chicken breasts
> 2 packs ready-cook egg noodles
> 1 medium carrot
> 4 spring onions
> ½ a red onion
> 8 small mushrooms
> 6-8 kale/spring green leaves
> 4 cloves garlic
> 1 handful of seeds
> 1 tsp Chinese five spice
> 1 tbsp low-salt soy sauce
> 1 tsp honey
> 1 tbsp rice vinegar
> 1 dstspn cooking oil

Method

1. Using a clean chopping board, thinly slice the chicken and place to one side. Wash your hands.
2. Now, using a different/clean board and knife, start to prepare your veggies; you can put them all in the same bowl before cooking as they will all be cooked together.
3. Peel and thinly the red onion.
4. Trim the spring onions by chopping off the root ends (hairy bit) and any scraggly bits on the opposite end if you wish (although these are usually perfectly edible). Once trimmed, slice your spring onions all the way through the middle length ways and then slice widthways to about 2-inch sized pieces.
5. Peel and grate the garlic and cauliflower (or chop finely). De-stalk your greens (see Pg. 14) and thinly slice into strips and thinly slice the mushrooms.
6. Peel the carrot and top and tail. Then make carrot ribbons, using the peeler.
7. Heat the oil in a medium-sized frying pan on a medium heat.
8. Add the five spice and mix well, then add the chicken and cook for about 3 minutes, turning regularly.
9. Add the veggies and mix well. Cook, stirring regularly for about 5 minutes. Then add the soy sauce, honey and rice vinegar. Mix well, then add about 1/3 mug water. Mix well.
10. Finally, add the noodles and cook for a further 2 minutes, stirring through the sauce.
11. ENJOY!

RAINBOW STIR FRY

Makes 4 portions

"Eat a rainbow" every day!

INGREDIENTS

> ¼ head of broccoli - florets
> ¼ small red cabbage
> ½ a red pepper
> ½ a yellow pepper
> 1 red onion
> 4 cloves garlic
> 1 carrot
> 2 serving spoon sweetcorn
> 1 tin of chickpeas
> 1 lime, juice and zest
> 1 dstspn low salt soy sauce
> 1 dash of hot sauce
> 2 nests flat rice noodles
> 1 dstspn cooking oil

METHOD

1. Prepare your vegetables - you can put them all in the same bowl before cooking as they will all be cooked together.
2. Thinly slice the red cabbage and thinly slice the broccoli florets, width ways so they still have the floret shape (like little flat trees!).
3. De-seed and thinly slice the peppers. Peel the carrot and top and tail. Then make carrot ribbons, using the peeler.
4. Peel and thinly slice the onion. Peel and grate the garlic.
5. Drain the chickpeas and rinse under cold water.
6. Zest the lime by grating on the smallest side of the grater. Then cut the lime in half and squeeze using a lemon squeezer.
7. Heat the oil in a medium-sized frying pan on a medium heat.
8. Add all the veggies and cook for about five minutes on a medium heat, stirring regularly.
9. Add the chickpeas, lime juice and zest, soy sauce and hot sauce and mix well.
10. Place the noodles in a saucepan and boil enough water (using a kettle as this is more economical) to cover them. Once boiled, add the water to the pan, cook on a medium heat for about 30-60 seconds.
11. Drain the noodles over the sink with a sieve, then add to your stir fry, along with the sweetcorn.
12. Toss everything together so that it is all mixed well and fully heated through.
13. ENJOY!

LEMON CHICKEN OR HALLOUMI STIR FRY

Makes 4 portions

This recipe is so easy and tastes amazing. Enjoy!

INGREDIENTS

> 2 chicken breasts or one block of halloumi
> 1 lemon, juice and zest
> 1 tsp honey
> 1 dstspn low-salt soy sauce
> 1 sachet miso soup
> 1 pinch of salt
> Thumb of ginger
> 4 cloves garlic
> 4 spring onion
> ½ red onion
> 1 green pepper
> 6-8 mushrooms
> Rice or noodles
> 1 dstspn cooking oil

METHOD

1. Make the marinade for the chicken/halloumi. In a large mug or small deep bowl add the honey, soy sauce and lemon juice and zest and give it a good stir using a metal spoon.

2. Next, using a clean chopping board, thinly slice the chicken – or cut the halloumi into chunks - and place it into the marinade, pushing it down with the spoon until it is completely covered. Wash your hands.

3. Now, using a different/clean board and knife, start to prepare your veggies; you can put them all in the same bowl before cooking as they will all be cooked together.

4. Peel and thinly slice the red onion, peel and grate the garlic, peel and grate the ginger.

5. Trim the spring onions by chopping off the root ends (hairy bit) and any scraggly bits on the opposite end if you wish (although these are usually perfectly edible). Once trimmed, slice your spring onions on a slant so that you have biggish oval-shaped discs.

6. De-seed and roughly large dice the peppers. I think it looks nice if the peppers are all slightly different shapes and sizes (no rules here!).

7. Cut the mushrooms into quarters.

8. Heat the oil in a medium-sized frying pan on a medium heat.

9. Using tongs or a spoon, remove the chicken from the marinade and add to the pan, cook for about 3 minutes, turning regularly.

10. Now add all the veggies and mix well. Then add about 1/3 mug water and the miso paste. Cook, stirring regularly for about 5 minutes.

11. Finally, add the chicken/halloumi marinade to the pan and toss everything together so that it is all mixed well and fully heated through.

12. Serve with a white and brown rice mix, noodles or couscous.

13. ENJOY!

Stews

TBC

CHICKPEA & PEPPER STEW

Makes 4 portions

Chickpeas are high in fibre and a great source of protein. This stew is warming and delightful, all year round.

INGREDIENTS

- 1 tin of tomatoes
- ½ an onion
- 2 balls of frozen spinach
- 3 cloves garlic
- ½ a red pepper
- ½ a yellow pepper
- ½ a green pepper
- (you can use frozen peppers too!)
- 1 tin of chickpeas
- 1 tsp caraway seeds
- 1 tsp dried coriander leaf
- 1 tsp smoked paprika
- 2 pinches of salt
- 200ml orange juice
- 1 dstspn cooking oil

METHOD

1. Peel and slice the onion.
2. Peel and grate or finely chop the garlic.
3. De-seed and slice the peppers.
4. Heat the oil in a medium-sized frying pan, on a medium heat. Then add the garlic, onion and peppers to the pan. Cook for one minute.
5. Add the coriander, salt, paprika, caraway and half a mug of water (about 100ml). Mix well.
6. Stir often for about five minutes.
7. Open the tin of chickpeas, drain in a sieve over the sink, and add to the pan, then add the tomatoes and orange juice. Bring to the boil, then turn the heat to medium low.
8. Add the spinach and stir well. As the spinach starts to defrost, you can start breaking it down using the back of a fork.
9. Cook for about ten minutes, or so, until the sauce starts to thicken.
10. Serve with a white and brown rice mix, pitta or couscous.
11. ENJOY!

CHICKEN STEW
Makes 4 portions

Chicken thighs, skin on, on the bone, are almost half the price of those with their skin off, off the bone! Also, the skin and bones are high in nutrition and add great flavour to this dish. Chicken is a lovely lean meat, high in protein and very nourishing. This stew is warming and delightful, all year round.

INGREDIENTS

> 4 chicken thighs, skin on, on the bone
> 4 cloves garlic
> 1 onion
> 2 carrots
> 1 tin of tomatoes
> 1 tsp smoked paprika
> 6 kale leaves/spring greens/ savoy cabbage
> ½ lemon, juice and zest
> 2 pinches of salt
> 1 dstspn cooking oil

METHOD

1. Zest and juice the lemon.
2. Peel and thinly slice the onion and peel and grate the garlic.
3. Peel the carrots, top and tail (by chopping off each end) and make ribbons using a peeler.
4. De-stalk and slice the kale/greens/cabbage (see Pg. 14), then thinly slice.
5. Heat the oil in a medium-sized deep sided sauce pan, on a medium heat. Then add the garlic, onion and salt to the pan. Mix well and cook for one minute.
6. Add the chicken thighs and cook for 2 minutes on each side – so that the skin is browned – add a tiny bit more oil if necessary.
7. Now remove the chicken and set to one side.
8. Add the carrots and greens to the pan, along with about half a mug of water (about 200 ml). Cook for two minutes.
9. Add the lemon juice and zest and the paprika and mix well.
10. Now put the chicken back in the pan. Try to make four holes in the veg so that the chicken is on the bottom of the pan and the veg is around and on top of the chicken.
11. Add the tin of tomatoes plus one tin again of water, bring to the boil, then turn the heat to low. If you have one, place a lid on the saucepan (no worries if not), and cook for 20-30 minutes.
12. Keep checking throughout the cooking process that your chicken isn't sticking to the pan and that there is still enough liquid covering the thighs.
13. You know your stew is cooked when the chicken meat falls easily off the bone and there is no red/pink around the bone.
14. Finally, take the thighs out of the stew, carefully, using a fork. Take off the skin and shred the meat off the bones. Then pop the meat back in the stew and mix it through the sauce. Alternatively, you can leave the thighs whole in the stew.
15. ENJOY!

Easy Read Recipes

MINESTRONE SOUP
Makes 4 servings

This Italian classic is a meal in itself, packed full of fibre and all your essential vitamins!

INGREDIENTS:

1 tin borlotti beans
1 tin tomatoes
1 carrot
2 celery sticks
2 handfuls spinach or 2 balls of frozen

	1 red onion
	3 cloves garlic
	1 tsp mixed herbs
	1 tsp dried basil
	1 tsp smoked paprika
	1 handful macaroni
	1 dstspn of cooking oil
	2 pinches of salt

800 ml water

METHOD:

1. Wash your hands.

2. Chop the carrot and celery into very small pieces.

3. Peel and thinly slice or chop the onion.

4. Peel and grate the garlic.

5. Add the oil to a medium-sized pan and place on your hob on a medium heat.

6. Place chopped carrot, celery, garlic and onion in the saucepan.

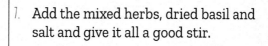

7. Add the mixed herbs, dried basil and salt and give it all a good stir.

8. Cook for about 5 minutes, stirring regularly.

9. Open the beans, drain into a sieve and rinse under cold water; add these to your saucepan.

10. Add the tinned tomatoes, the water and macaroni to the saucepan.

11. Using a wooden spoon, break down the tomatoes in the pan by pushing and stirring the ingredients.

12. Add the spinach and paprika.

13. Give it all a good stir and turn your hob to a medium low heat.

14. Until the liquid is boiling slowly.

15. Stir regularly.

16. Cook the soup for about ten minutes, stirring regularly, until the macaroni is soft.

17. ENJOY!

PEA & MINT SOUP
Makes 4 servings

Don't underestimate the mighty pea! These little powerhouses are packed with vitamin C and bursting with natural sugars. Mint is good for your digestion and will grow anywhere in abundance! Together these two are a match made in heaven and this recipe is so easy, you can make a batch and throw it in the freezer for a rainy day.

INGREDIENTS:

1 red onion
2 cloves garlic
1 tsp mixed herbs
1 sachet of miso soup paste
1 dstspn of cooking oil

2 pinches of salt
800 ml water
A handful of fresh mint
3 big spoons of frozen peas

METHOD:

1. Wash your hands.
2. Chop the mint as small as you can. You may want to use scissors.
3. Peel and chop the onion.

4. Peel and chop the garlic.

5. Add the oil to a medium-sized saucepan.

6. Place on your hob on a medium heat and add the onion and garlic.

7. Add the mixed herbs, dried basil and salt and give it all a good stir.

8. Turn the heat to low.

9. Add the miso paste.

10. Stir well.

11. Add the mint and peas.

12. Stir well.

13. Cook, until the soup is hot.

14. Stir regularly.

15. You can then blend your soup using a stick blender, or mash with a potato masher.

16. Add extra water if the soup is too thick and stir well.

17. **ENJOY!**

TOMATO & SWEET POTATO SOUP
Makes 4 servings

Sweet potatoes are rich in beta-carotene, which is converted by the body into the essential vitamin A, supporting eye health, skin health and your immune system. They are also a great source of fibre.

INGREDIENTS:

1 red onion	
4 cloves garlic	
1 tsp mixed herbs	
1 tsp smoked paprika (optional)	
1 tin of tomatoes	

1 dstspn of cooking oil
1 pinch of salt
500 ml water
1 medium-sized sweet potato

METHOD:

1. Wash your hands.
2. Peel and chop the onion and garlic so it is really small.
3. Peel the sweet potato. 4. Chop the sweet potato into small pieces.

5. Add the oil to a medium sized saucepan.

6. Place on your hob on a medium heat and add the onion and garlic.

7. Add the mixed herbs and salt and give it all a good stir.

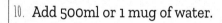

8. Add the sweet potato.

9. Stir well.

10. Add 500ml or 1 mug of water.

11. Add the tomatoes.

12. Turn your hob to a high heat.

13. When it starts to bubble a lot, turn to a medium heat. Cook until the potatoes are soft.

14. You can then blend your soup using a stick blender, or mash with a potato masher.

15. Add extra water if the soup is too thick and stir well.

16. **ENJOY!**

CAJUN BLACK BEAN BURRITO

Serves 1; double up ingredients as necessary to enjoy with others.

Classic summer flavours for early evening sharing.

INGREDIENTS:

	1 handful of spinach
	1 large spoon of Cajun black bean mix
	2 spoons of coleslaw
	1 handful of rice (white & brown mix is best)
	1 dash hot sauce

A small piece of cheese
1 tortilla wrap
You will also need some tin foil.

METHOD:

1. Wash your hands.
2. First put the rice on to cook in a medium saucepan, on a medium heat.   3. The water should cover the rice.
4. While the rice is cooking, grate the cheese.
5. Roll out the tin foil then place the wrap on top of the rolled out flat piece of foil.   6. Tear the foil off the roll so you have a wrap-sized square.

7. Once the rice is cooked, drain, using a sieve, and cool under cold running water for 30 seconds.

8. Now you can assemble your burrito (see Pg. 40).

9. Finally, using a clean frying pan, on a low to medium heat, place your burrito in the pan, and "dry fry" (no oil).

10. Turn each side to the heat for about 30 seconds, until all sides of the foil are warm - almost too hot to touch.

11. ENJOY!

COLESLAW

INGREDIENTS:

	1 red onion
	¼ red cabbage
	2 medium carrots
	1 spoon of mayonnaise
	1 spoon of plain yogurt

METHOD:

1. Wash your hands.
2. Now peel and grate the carrot.
3. Peel the onion and slice as thin as you can.
4. Slice the cabbage as thin as you can.
5. Add all your vegetable to a mixing bowl.   6. Add the yogurt and mayonnaise.   7. Mix well.
8. ENJOY!

CAJUN BLACK BEAN MIX

INGREDIENTS:

1 red onion
2 cloves garlic
1 tin of black beans
1 tin of tomatoes
2 tsp Cajun spice

1 medium spoon of cooking oil

METHOD:

1. Wash your hands.

2. Peel and chop the onion and garlic so it is really small.

3. Add the oil to a medium sized saucepan.

4. Place on your hob on a medium heat.

5. Add the onion and garlic and mix well.

6. Cook until it starts to sizzle.

7. Then add the black beans and the Cajun spice.

8. Mix well.

9. Then add the tomatoes.

10. Mix well.

11. Turn to a low heat and cook for about ten minutes.

12. Stir regularly and break down the beans using a fork.

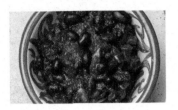

13. ENJOY!

ROASTED SWEET POTATO

INGREDIENTS:

1 dessert spoon of cooking oil
1 pinch of salt
2 medium-sized sweet potatoes

METHOD:

1. Wash your hands.

2. Peel the sweet potato.

3. Chop the sweet potato into small pieces.

4. Add the oil to a medium sized baking dish.

5. Add the salt.

6. Add the chopped sweet potato.

7. Mix well

8. Cook in the oven at a medium to high heat for about 15 minutes or until the potato is soft.

9. Remember to use oven gloves when removing the baking tray from the oven.

10. ENJOY!

TOMATO SALSA

INGREDIENTS:

4 salad tomatoes
½ a red onion
4 cloves garlic
1 lime
1 teaspoon of dried coriander

METHOD:

1. Wash your hands.

2. Peel and chop the onion and garlic so it is really small.

3. Chop the tomatoes small.

4. First zest the lime by grating it on the smallest side of the grater.

5. Then cut the lime in half and squeeze using a lemon squeezer.

6. Add all the ingredients to a mixing bowl and mix well.

7. If possible, leave for about 1 hour to let all the flavours happen ☺

8. ENJOY!

BLACK BEAN & SPINACH QUESADILLA

Serves 1; double up ingredients as necessary to enjoy with others.

INGREDIENTS:

A small piece of cheese
1 tortilla wrap
1 handful of spinach
1 large spoon of Cajun black bean mix
1 teaspoon of cooking oil

METHOD:

1. Wash your hands.

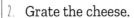

2. Grate the cheese.

3. Now, place your wrap onto a chopping board.

4. Then, using a knife, cut from the centre of the wrap in a straight line to the outside edge of the wrap (see *How to Fold your Quesadilla*, Pg. 41).

5. Place all the ingredients across the surface of the wrap.

6. Then, fold in half and half again.

7. Then heat a dash of oil in a frying pan on a medium heat.

8. Carefully lift your quesadilla into the pan and fry gently, turning – using a fish slice - so that each side reaches a nice golden-brown crispiness.

9. ENJOY!

SWEET POTATO & SWEETCORN QUESADILLA

Serves 1; double up ingredients as necessary to enjoy with others.

Filling and satisfying – this burrito is comfort food at its best and full of fibre too.

INGREDIENTS:

	A small piece of cheese
	1 tortilla wrap (wholemeal is best).
	1 handful of spinach
	2 dessert spoons of frozen sweetcorn
	1 dessert spoon of tomato salsa (recipe Pg. 60)

1 large spoon of roasted sweet potato (see recipe, Pg. 63)
1 teaspoon of cooking oil

METHOD:

1.	Wash your hands.
2.	Pop your sweetcorn in mug of hot tap water for a few minutes to defrost.
3.	Now grate the cheese.
4.	Now, place your wrap onto a chopping board.
5.	Then, using a knife, cut from the centre of the wrap in a straight line to the outside edge of the wrap (see *How to Fold your Quesadilla*, Pg. 41).
6.	Place all the ingredients across the surface of the wrap.
7.	Then, fold in half and half again.

8. Then heat a dash of oil in a frying pan on a medium heat.

9. Carefully lift your quesadilla into the pan and fry gently, turning – using a fish slice - so that each side reaches a nice golden-brown crispiness.

10. ENJOY!

CHICKEN CURRY

It's a classic! In this curry, for simplicity we use a curry paste. As you continue through this section you will learn how easy it is to make your own. Homemade curries are a great way to use up what's in the fridge and are really good for you.

INGREDIENTS:

1 red pepper	
1 yellow pepper	
1 green pepper	
1 tin of tomatoes	
1 dessert spoon of hot curry paste	

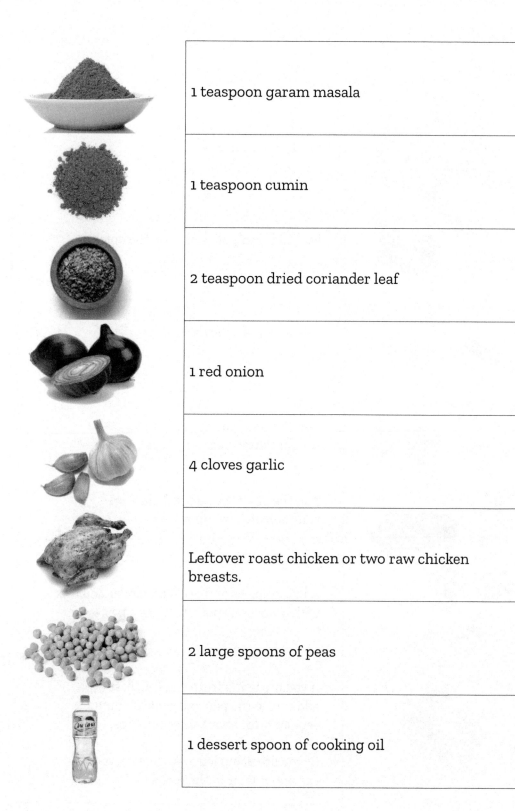

1 teaspoon garam masala
1 teaspoon cumin
2 teaspoon dried coriander leaf
1 red onion
4 cloves garlic
Leftover roast chicken or two raw chicken breasts.
2 large spoons of peas
1 dessert spoon of cooking oil

METHOD:

1. Wash your hands.
2. Peel and thinly slice or chop the onion.
3. Peel and grate the garlic.
4. Next, de-seed the peppers and roughly large dice.
5. Add the oil to the pan and place on your hob on a medium heat.
6. Add the spices and dried coriander and mix with a wooden spoon to make a paste.
7. If you are using fresh chicken, first add this to the pan and cook, turning regularly, for about three minutes. 8. (If you are using leftover chicken, you can add it later in the recipe).

9. Now add the onion and garlic and cook for two minutes.

10. Now add the peppers and cook for two minutes.

11. Now add one third of a mug of water, stir well and cook for five minutes.

12. Add the curry paste and the tomatoes and mix well.

13. Cook until the peppers are soft.

14. Use a masher to break down the sauce.

15. Finally add the peas and leftover chicken (if using).

16. Give it all a good stir and cook for a further two minutes.

17. Serve with rice, couscous, naan bread or pitta bread.

18. ENJOY!

SWEET POTATO CURRY
Makes 4 portions

Sweet potatoes are rich in beta-carotene, which is converted by the body into the essential vitamin A, supporting eye health, skin health and your immune system. They are also a great source of fibre.

INGREDIENTS:

	2 medium-sized sweet potatoes
	1 tin of tomatoes
	1 dessert spoon of medium or hot curry powder
	1 teaspoon garam masala
	1 teaspoon cumin

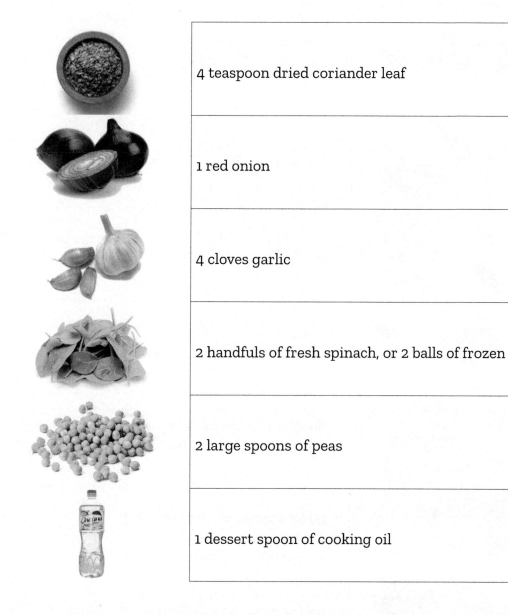

	4 teaspoon dried coriander leaf
	1 red onion
	4 cloves garlic
	2 handfuls of fresh spinach, or 2 balls of frozen
	2 large spoons of peas
	1 dessert spoon of cooking oil

METHOD:

1. Wash your hands.

2. Peel your potatoes and cut into small cubes.

3. Peel and chop the onion really small.

4. Peel and grate the garlic.

5. Chop the spinach into thin strips.

6. Add the oil to the pan and place on your hob on a medium heat.

7. Add the spices, curry powder and dried coriander and mix with a wooden spoon to make a paste.

8. Now add the onion and garlic and cook for two minutes.

9. Now add the chopped sweet potato and cook for two minutes. Stir regularly.

10. Add the tinned tomatoes and then fill the tin again with water – to get all the lovely juice – and add this to the pan as well.

11. Turn the heat to medium high, bring to the boil. Turn the heat back to medium and cook for about 15 minutes, or until the potatoes are soft, adding more water if necessary (enough to keep a thick sauce consistency).

12. Add peas and spinach and stir for about five minutes, until everything is hot.

13. Serve with rice, couscous, naan bread or pitta bread.

14. ENJOY!

BEETROOT CURRY

Makes 4 portions

Ahh, the super beet! Beetroot is a great source of fibre, iron and vitamin C. They are easy to grow and will sit happily in the ground, long into the autumn. When in season they can be found quite cheaply at farmers' markets and will freeze well (cook and freeze in batches).

INGREDIENTS:

4 medium-sized beetroot
1 tin of tomatoes
1 dessert spoon of medium or hot curry paste
1 teaspoon caraway seeds
1 teaspoon cumin

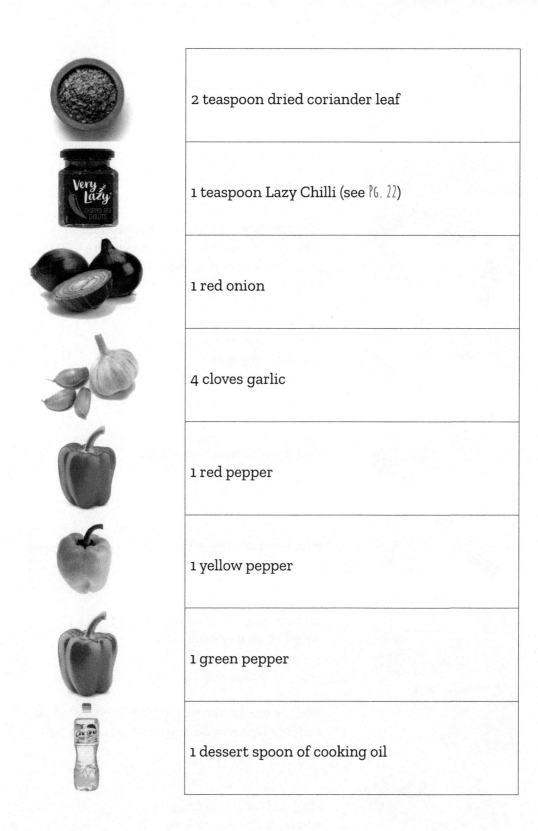

	2 teaspoon dried coriander leaf
	1 teaspoon Lazy Chilli (see PG. 22)
	1 red onion
	4 cloves garlic
	1 red pepper
	1 yellow pepper
	1 green pepper
	1 dessert spoon of cooking oil

METHOD:

1. Wash your hands.

2. Peel and dice the beetroot and set aside – be warned, the juice gets everywhere (but don't worry, it doesn't stain!) You may also want to wear gloves.

3. Next, de-seed the peppers and roughly large dice.

4. Peel and thinly slice the onion.

5. Peel and grate the garlic.

6. Add the oil to the pan and place on your hob on a medium heat.

7. Add the spices, curry paste and dried coriander and mix with a wooden spoon to make a paste.

8. Now add the onion and garlic and cook for two minutes.

9. Now add the peppers and cook for two minutes. Stir regularly.

10. Now add your beetroot and the Lazy Chilli.

11. Mix well.

12. Add the tinned tomatoes and then fill the tin again with water – to get all the lovely juice – and add this to the pan as well.

13. Turn the heat to medium high, bring to the boil. Turn the heat back to medium and cook for about 15 minutes, or until the beetroot is soft, adding more water if necessary (enough to keep a thick sauce consistency).

14. Serve with rice, couscous, naan bread or pitta bread.

15. ENJOY!

BASE TOMATO SAUCE

Makes 4-6 portions - can double as tomato soup!

Shop-bought pasta sauce is high in salt and added sugars. By making your own you are in control of what goes in. This sauce can be made in large batches and frozen in portions. It's a great base for soups, stews, curries, pastas and pizza. We use carrots in our tomato sauce as a great way to sneak in extra veggies and also add sweetness.

INGREDIENTS:

2 medium carrots
2 tins of tomatoes
1 red onion
4 cloves garlic
2 teaspoons of mixed herbs

2 pinches of salt
1 dessert spoon of honey
1 dessert spoon of cooking oil

METHOD:

1.	Wash your hands.
2.	Peel the onion and chop it really small.
3.	Peel and grate the garlic.
4.	Peel the carrots. Cut each end off. Then grate.

5. Add the oil to the pan and place on your hob on a medium heat.

6. Add the salt and mixed herbs and give it all a good stir.

7. Now add the onion and garlic and cook for two minutes.

8. Add the tinned tomatoes and then fill the tins again with water – to get all the lovely juice – and add this to the pan as well.

9. Add the honey, mix well, and cook for about 30 seconds.

10. You can then blend your sauce using a stick blender or mash with a potato masher for a chunkier texture.

11. If your sauce is too thick add a little extra water.

12. You can use your sauce as a base for pastas, curries, pizza, soups and stews!

13. ENJOY!

SUMMER VEGETABLE PASTA
Makes 4 portions

INGREDIENTS:

2 handfuls of wild garlic (see PG. 93)
2 handfuls of fresh spinach
2 handfuls of fresh mint (optional)
2 handfuls of fresh basil (optional)
3 salad tomatoes

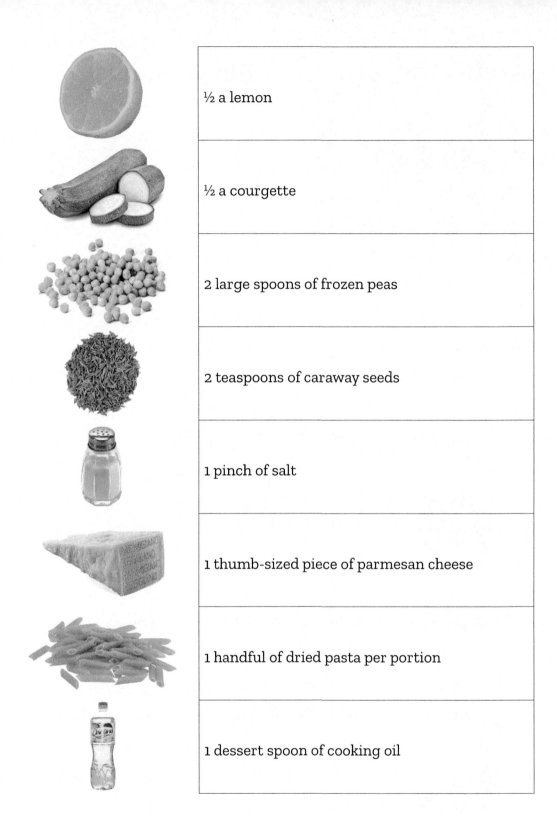

	½ a lemon
	½ a courgette
	2 large spoons of frozen peas
	2 teaspoons of caraway seeds
	1 pinch of salt
	1 thumb-sized piece of parmesan cheese
	1 handful of dried pasta per portion
	1 dessert spoon of cooking oil

METHOD:

1. Wash your hands.

2. Precook your pasta, cool and set aside.

3. Wash the wild garlic and spinach thoroughly.

4. Squeeze the lemon and set the juice aside.

5. Now, using scissors, roughly cut up the mint, basil, wild garlic and spinach so that they are in small strips.

6. Now chop the tomatoes into small cubes.

7. Zest the lemon rind, using the smallest grating blade

8. Peel the courgette into ribbons

9. Place all your prepared veg and lemon zest into a mixing bowl.

10. Add the peas, caraway seeds and salt, and mix well.

11. Add the oil to the pan and place on your hob on a medium heat.

12. Now add the contents of your mixing bowl to the pan and mix well.

13. Add the lemon juice and cook for about three minutes, stirring continuously.

14. Add the cooked pasta to the pan and mix well.

15. Finally, grate the parmesan straight into the pan and mix well for about 30 seconds.

16. ENJOY!

VIBRANT TUNA PASTA
Makes 4 portions

This dish screams summer! Full of colour and flavour it's an easy peasy family favourite.

INGREDIENTS:

	1 red pepper
	1 yellow pepper
	1 tin of tomatoes
	2 large spoons of frozen sweetcorn
	2 handfuls of fresh spinach or 2 balls of frozen

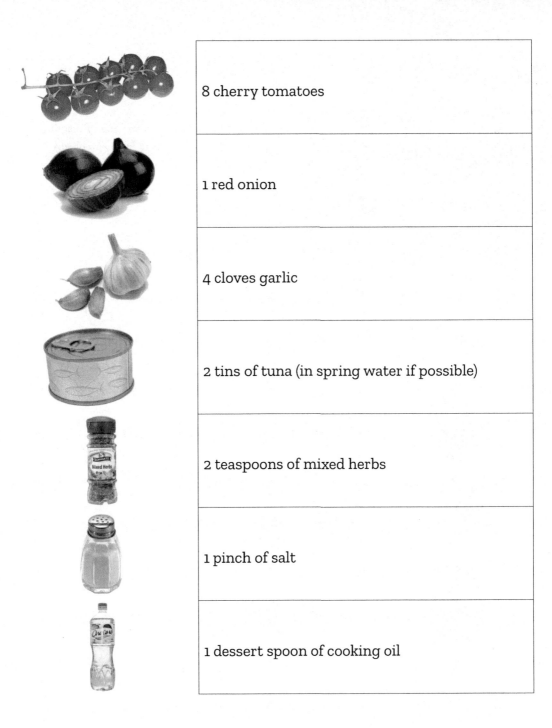

	8 cherry tomatoes
	1 red onion
	4 cloves garlic
	2 tins of tuna (in spring water if possible)
	2 teaspoons of mixed herbs
	1 pinch of salt
	1 dessert spoon of cooking oil

METHOD:

1. Wash your hands.

2. Peel the onion and chop it really small.

3. Peel and grate the garlic.

4. Next, de-seed the peppers and roughly large dice.

5. Add the oil to the pan and place on your hob on a medium heat.

6. Add the salt and mixed herbs and give it all a good stir.

7. Now add the onion and garlic and cook for one minute.

8. Add the peppers. Cook for three minutes, stirring regularly.

9. Add the tinned tomatoes and then fill the tin again with water – to get all the lovely juice – and add this to the pan as well.

10. Mix well.

11. Finally, add the tuna, spinach and sweetcorn.

12. Cook for about five minutes, breaking down any frozen spinach with a fork.

13. Serve with pasta.

14. ENJOY!

SPRING VEGETABLE RISOTTO
Makes 4-6 portions

This essential immune-boosting risotto uses all the greens, giving you a hit of vitamins K and C, keeping your blood and heart healthy. It tastes clean, fresh and delicious.

INGREDIENTS:

2 handfuls of fresh spinach or 2 balls of frozen
1 handful of wild garlic
1 handful of fresh rocket
1 handful of fresh mint
2 large spoons of frozen peas

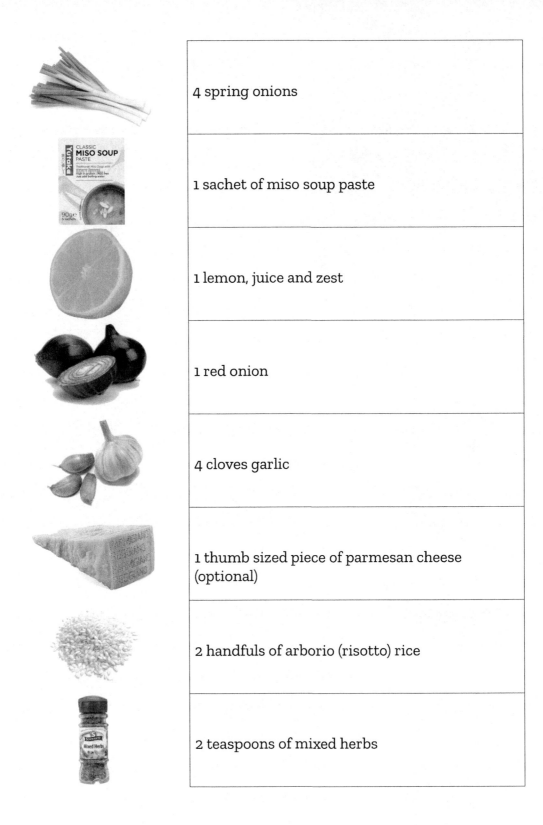

	4 spring onions
	1 sachet of miso soup paste
	1 lemon, juice and zest
	1 red onion
	4 cloves garlic
	1 thumb sized piece of parmesan cheese (optional)
	2 handfuls of arborio (risotto) rice
	2 teaspoons of mixed herbs

1 pinch of salt
1 dessert spoon of cooking oil
1 litre of water

METHOD:

1. Wash your hands.
2. Peel the onion and chop it really small.
3. Peel and grate the garlic.

4. Now, trim the spring onions by chopping off the root ends (hairy bit) and any scraggly bits on the opposite end if you wish (although these are usually perfectly edible).

5. Once trimmed, slice your spring onions on a slant so that you have biggish oval-shaped discs.

6. If you are using fresh spinach, roughly chop (or use scissors) and set to one side.

7. If you are using frozen spinach pop it in a mug of hot water to defrost and separate with a fork (this takes about two minutes).

8. Thoroughly wash and then roughly chop (or use scissors) the wild garlic.

9. Juice and zest the lemon rind (using the smallest blade on the grater, page

10. Boil 800 ml water in your kettle, put it in a jug or bowl then add 200ml cold water. Add the miso soup paste and mix well.

11. Add the oil to the pan and place on your hob on a medium heat.

12. Add the salt and mixed herbs and give it all a good stir.

13. Now add the onion and garlic and cook for two minutes.

14. Now add the rice and mix well.

15. Now add one ladle (or cup) of this water to the rice.

16. Cook on a medium to low heat until the water has all disappeared into the rice, then add another ladle/mug of water.

17. Repeat this process until the rice is soft, but with a 'bite'.

18. Finally - near the end of the rice cooking process – add the spinach, peas, lemon juice and zest, wild garlic, mint and rocket, stirring through the rice until the greens have gone a darker green and are soft.

19. Serve with parmesan if desired.

20. ENJOY!

RAINBOW STIR FRY

Makes 4 portions

"Eat a rainbow" every day!

INGREDIENTS:

½ a head of broccoli (about 6 florets)
½ a small red cabbage
½ a red pepper
½ a yellow pepper
1 carrot

	2 large spoons of frozen sweetcorn
	1 red onion
	4 cloves garlic
	1 lime
	1 tin of chickpeas, drained
	1 dessert spoon of low salt soy sauce
	1 dash hot sauce
	2 nests of flat rice noodles

1 dessert spoon of cooking oil

METHOD:

1. Wash your hands.
2. Prepare your vegetables. You can put them all in the same bowl before cooking as they will all be cooked together.

3. Thinly slice the red cabbage.
4. Thinly slice the broccoli florets, width ways so they still have the floret shape (like little flat trees!).

5. Next, de-seed the peppers and thinly slice.

6. Peel and chop the onion and garlic so it is really small.
7. Peel the carrot, chop the ends off and make carrot ribbons, using a peeler

8. Drain the chickpeas and rinse under cold water.

9. Zest the lime by grating on the smallest side of the grater.

10. Then cut the lime in half and squeeze using a lemon squeezer.

11. Add the oil to the pan and place on your hob on a medium heat.

12. Add all the veggies and cook for about five minutes on a medium heat, stirring regularly.

13. Then add the chickpeas, lime juice and zest, soy sauce and hot sauce and mix well.

14. Now place the noodles in a saucepan and boil enough water (using a kettle as this is more economical) to cover them.

15. Once boiled, add the water to the pan, cook on a medium heat for about 30-60 seconds.

16. Drain the noodles over the sink with a sieve.

17. Then add to your veggies in the pan.

18. Add the sweetcorn too.

19. Stir everything together so that it is all mixed well and thoroughly heated through.

20. ENJOY!

FAJITAS

Makes 4 portions

Fajitas are usually an absolute winner with all the family. Quick and easy to make, full of great nutrition and a great way to use up leftover bits and bobs in the fridge.

INGREDIENTS:

4 wholemeal wraps
1 red pepper
1 yellow pepper
1 red onion
2 handfuls of fresh spinach

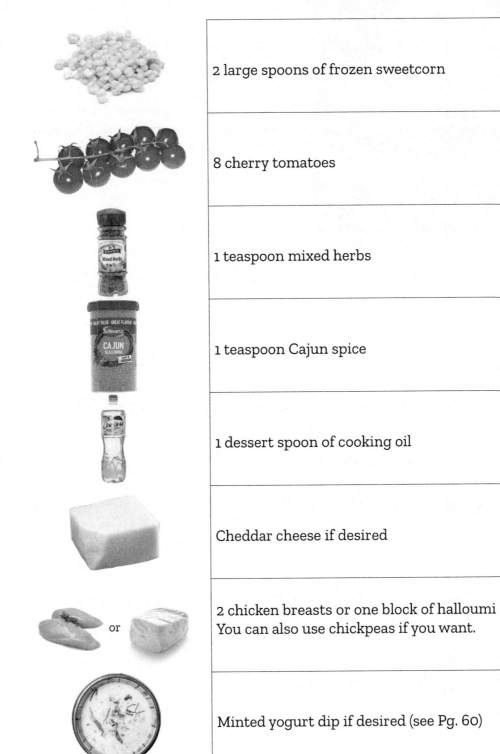

	2 large spoons of frozen sweetcorn
	8 cherry tomatoes
	1 teaspoon mixed herbs
	1 teaspoon Cajun spice
	1 dessert spoon of cooking oil
	Cheddar cheese if desired
or	2 chicken breasts or one block of halloumi You can also use chickpeas if you want.
	Minted yogurt dip if desired (see Pg. 60)

METHOD:

1.	Wash your hands.
2.	Using a clean chopping board, thinly slice the chicken – or cut the halloumi into chunks.
3.	Then wash your hands.
4.	Using a clean or different chopping board,
5.	De-seed the peppers and thinly slice.
6.	Cut the tomatoes in half and set aside.
7.	Add the oil to the pan and place on your hob on a medium heat.
8.	Add the mixed herbs, Cajun spice, peppers and onions, mix well and cook for about two minutes.
9.	Then add the chicken or halloumi, stirring through the veg, and cook for a further five minutes, turning regularly.
10.	Finally, add the tomatoes, spinach and sweetcorn; mix well and stir, cook for another two minutes.

11. When this is done, take your wraps, add a thin layer of yogurt dip (if using),and spread across the wrap. Add the chicken/halloumi & veg mix and a little grated cheese if desired, wrap, folding in the sides, and eat!

12. ENJOY!

SMOKY LENTIL AND SWEET POTATO CHILLI

Makes 4 portions

If you've never made your own chilli, now is the time to start. This recipe is easy, vegan, fibrous and as hot as you like! Enjoy!

INGREDIENTS:

1 red onion
4 cloves garlic
1 red pepper
1 medium-sized sweet potato
1 tin of black beans

	2 handfuls of split red lentils
	1 tsp cumin
	1 tsp smoked paprika
	2 pinches of salt
	1 dessert spoon of Lazy Chilli
	1 dessert spoon of cooking oil

METHOD:

1. Wash your hands.

2. Peel and chop the onion.

3. Peel and grate the garlic.

4. Next, de-seed the peppers and thinly slice.

5. Peel your potatoes and cut into small cubes.

6. Add the oil to the pan and place on your hob on a medium heat.

7. Then add the garlic, onion, peppers and sweet potato to the pan, mix well so the veggies are coated in oil.

8. Then add the cumin, paprika, chilli and salt, mix well and cook for two minutes.

9. Add a splash of water.

10. Mix well and cook for two minutes.

11. Then add the whole tin of black beans and two handfuls of red lentils.

12. Cook until the lentils and sweet potato are soft, adding more water through the cooking process if necessary.

13. Serve with a white and brown rice mix, pitta bread or couscous.

14. ENJOY!

Printed in Great Britain
by Amazon

37422332R00110